# A FalconGuide® to Death Valley National Park

## Help Us Keep This Guide Up to Date

Every effort has been made by the authors and editors to make this guide as accurate and useful as possible. However, many things can change after a guide is published—roads close, regulations change, trails are rerouted, and so on.

We would love to hear from you concerning your experiences with this guide and how you feel it could be made better and be kept up to date. While we may not be able to respond to all comments and suggestions, we'll take them to heart and we'll also make certain to share them with the authors. Please send your comments and suggestions to the following address:

The Globe Pequot Press
Reader Response/Editorial Department
P.O. Box 480
Guilford, CT 06437

Or you may e-mail us at:
editorial@GlobePequot.com

Thanks for your input, and happy travels!

A **FALCON** GUIDE ®

*Exploring Series*

# A FalconGuide® to Death Valley National Park

## A Guide to Exploring the Great Outdoors

### Bert and Jane Gildart

FALCON®

GUILFORD, CONNECTICUT
HELENA, MONTANA
AN IMPRINT OF THE GLOBE PEQUOT PRESS

**A FALCON GUIDE ®**

For Dad, with much gratitude for help over the years

# Acknowledgments

No book is ever truly completed without the help of others, and that is certainly true in this case. From start to finish, many people stepped in to furnish us with information and tidbits. To all of you, many thanks.

We'd like to particularly acknowledge our front-line readers from Death Valley National Park: Terry Baldino, Assistant Chief of Interpretation, for time spent reading the manuscript and for his thoughtful suggestions. To old friend, great editor, and longtime Death Valley devotee, Ed Rothfus, we are grateful for your time with red pen and good ideas. And to Ranger Charlie Callagan, thanks for answering our many questions. We'd also like to thank the good folks at The Globe Pequot Press for their patience, editing, and many suggestions. And last, but not least, gratitude to the many wonderful friends we met in Death Valley who provided us with vignettes of their own.

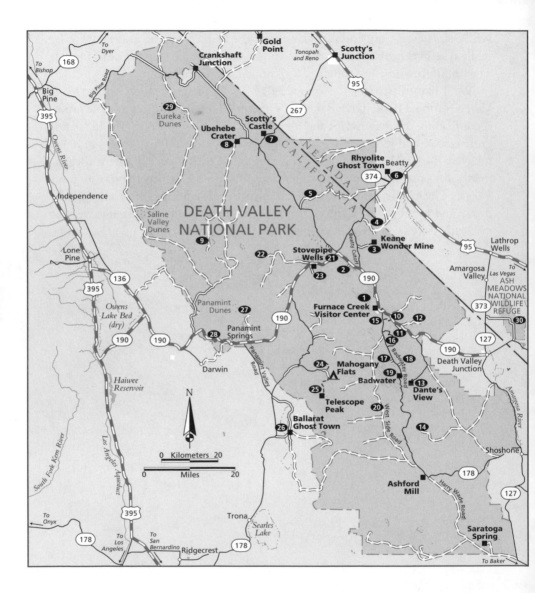

To Dyer
To Bishop
168
Big Pine
395
Big Pine Road
Independence
Owens River
Lone Pine
136
395
Owens Lake Bed (dry)
190
190
Haiwee Reservoir
South Fork Kern River
Los Angeles Aqueduct
395
To Onyx
178
To Los Angeles
To San Bernardino
Ridgecrest
178
Trona
Searles Lake

Crankshaft Junction
Gold Point
To Tonopah and Reno
Scotty's Junction
95
267
29 Eureka Dunes
Ubehebe Crater 8
Scotty's Castle 7
NEVADA CALIFORNIA
Rhyolite Ghost Town
Beatty
374 6
5
4
DEATH VALLEY NATIONAL PARK
Saline Valley Dunes
9
22
Stovepipe Wells 21
23 2
Keane Wonder Mine
3
190
95
Lathrop Wells
Amargosa Valley
ASH MEADOWS NATIONAL WILDLIFE REFUGE
To Las Vegas
373
Panamint Dunes
27
190
Panamint Springs 28
190
1
Furnace Creek Visitor Center
15
10
12
30
127
Darwin
24
Mahogany Flats
Badwater 19
16
11
17 18
190
Death Valley Junction
13
Dante's View
25
Telescope Peak
20
West Side Road
Amargosa River
Shoshone
Ballarat Ghost Town 26
14
178
127
N
0 Kilometers 20
0 Miles 20
Panamint Valley Road
Badwater Road
Ashford Mill
Harry Wade Road
178
Saratoga Spring
To Baker

# Contents

## Hikes and Drives East of the Park—In Nevada

## Death Valley National Park: Land of Great Mystery

In Death Valley, not far from Badwater, California (an expanse of foul-tasting water and dreadful land that is also the lowest point in the Western Hemisphere), there extends a forbidding landscape officially known as the Devil's Golf Course. Throughout the year, many days in this area are very hot, still, and unearthly quiet.

One January day several years ago, we walked into this jagged land and heard sounds during lulls in our conversation. Pausing and cupping our ears, we listened. All around us, the ground spoke: It snapped, it crackled, and it popped.

Although the sound emanated from beneath our feet, the cause remained a mystery until Ranger/Naturalist Charlie Callagan enlightened us at an evening program. Callagan explained that the sounds were the results of the incredibly dry air sucking every last drop of moisture from the chalky landscape. The friction of salt granule against collapsed salt granule created the snapping, cracking, and popping. Intriguing as that phenomenon proved to be, we also learned that it was just one of the park's many mysteries.

According to Callagan, Death Valley National Park has a river that disappears and a strange fish species whose egress is choked off from other water sources. (How'd they get here, and how do they survive—and thrive—in this unique saltwater environment?) And that's just for openers. The park has rocks that move, sands that sing, historical characters who bamboozled their followers at every turn, and world-class geological features that lure appreciative scientists from all over the world. Death Valley has phenomenally hot temperatures; in fact, it has the world's hottest official *average* temperatures. Arguably, it may also have the world's hottest temperature reading.

This entire area is unquestionably a land of great mystery, beauty, and endless intrigue, and its features are infused with a fascinating array of plants and animals whose very existence here seems tenuous at best. It is this tome of inscrutability, with chapters still to be written, that continues to lure back a dedicated and faithful following.

Death Valley was established in 1933 as a national monument by Pres. Herbert Hoover. At the time, Death Valley National Monument comprised a 2,036,000-acre expanse of land that even then bisected massive mountain ranges.

*Devils Golf Course—a place where things snap, crackle, and pop.*

In 1994 the monument was dramatically increased by virtue of the California Desert Protection Act under the Clinton Administration. Congress provided the additional lands with environmental protection and changed the status of the monument to national park. Today, at 3,396,000 acres, Death Valley is the largest national park outside Alaska. To be applauded is the fact that 95 percent of the park was officially declared wilderness in 76 different areas, some contiguous, some not. These areas join a beleaguered remnant of only 1 percent of the nation's lands (all of which were once de facto wilderness) that enjoy protection under the 1967 Wilderness Act. What that means in practical terms is that those who want to use off-road vehicles must go elsewhere—to one of the many other areas in California where such use is sanctioned. Death Valley National Park does not permit the use of off-road vehicles anywhere except on designated backcountry roads, and then all vehicles and their drivers must be licensed. What that means for those who hike into the desert is that they can expect to find the same types of conditions that so many early explorers—and even early prospectors—encountered. Essentially, early Death Valley visitors encountered raw desert, specifically the Mojave and Great Basin Deserts, which together cover parts of Nevada, Utah, Arizona, California, and New Mexico. Some say, that Death Valley celebrates the very best these two ecosystems have to offer.

By definition, deserts are areas that receive less than 10 inches of rainfall annually. Death Valley surpasses that standard. Vast regions of the park receive less than 1.5 inches of rain a year. Death Valley is as dry as parchment paper. In fact, some plants here respond to the touch as though they were just that. Still, despite the apparent scarcity of water, Indians who once roamed this area knew there was no place in the valley more than 15 miles from potable surface water. That does not mean, however, that *you* will be able to find water or that a 15-mile search in the summer heat looking for water won't transform you into something resembling a prune. Nor does it mean that you can embark on a hike (even a short one!) without adequate water. Tragically, in 2001 a hiker perished less than a mile from the trailhead near Zabriskie Point. He died of heat stroke, resulting from a lack of water.

Because of the park's vagaries—and immensity—your first and most productive stop will be the visitor center located immediately adjacent to Furnace Creek Campground. Here rangers catch you up on the park's current events, offer precautionary advice, and suggest areas to visit—all of which we've further elaborated on in this book.

One area all naturalists suggest visiting is the park's sand dunes. Because of the Desert Protection Act, the park now contains five such dunes. The ones most easily accessible are the Death Valley Dunes, or Mesquite Flat Dunes, near Stove Pipe Wells—a settlement established when someone discovered a spring and stuck a stovepipe into the soil to mark the location of the well in the shifting sand.

The best time to visit the dunes is just after the coyotes have started yipping, when it is cool and the light is dramatic. At such times, bold shadows leap out and reveal a multitude of nocturnal stories. In one area you may see where a sidewinder has looped its way across the sand. Intermingled with these lines may be the tracks of a kangaroo rat. Sometimes these tracks end abruptly (we'll have more to say about that later). Other dunes can offer equally as fascinating outings and are worth exploring. Naturalists conduct hikes to the dunes near Stovepipe Wells, and these hikes are worth checking out. In fact, there are many such hikes, which we've summarized in Appendix A.

The park also offers a number of drives, on both paved and unpaved roads, and one of the easiest departs from Stovepipe Wells. Just past the dunes and the motel-store complex, the road ascends into the Panamint Mountains. The drive is particularly enjoyable in late spring, when afternoon temperatures climb into the 90s. The road takes you to the Charcoal Kilns and from here provides access to the Telescope Peak trailhead. The trail climbs 7 miles past stands of bristlecone pines (the oldest living tree species in the world) and takes you to the 11,049-foot-high mountaintop. From here you can look down on Badwater and enjoy some of the greatest vertical relief in all North America.

For those who don't wish to hike, there are many alternatives. If you're still in the Panamint Mountains in the vicinity of the Charcoal Kilns, explore them; they provide an interesting look into the history of several precious metals. Kilns were used to convert wood from the nearby piñon pines into charcoal. The charcoal provided the high heat needed to separate silver from sulfur, an element with which it is usually associated in nature.

The park also provides many other looks into Death Valley's mining history. Below the Charcoal Kilns—back near Furnace Creek—there's the Borax Museum. Not far from the museum, there's a well-preserved site where some of the great twenty-mule-team wagons were once used to transport borax (called "white gold") to the railhead at Mojave. These treks eventually provided the romantic backdrop for Pacific Coast Borax's TV series, *Death Valley Days*, popular in the 1950s. Various interpretive programs provide detailed insights, so dig in; many of today's ghost towns in and immediately around the park owe their existence to borax, gold, silver, and lead. So, too, do the many characters whose histories have become legend. We've provided a lexicon on those who did much to make the compound so famous. Shorty Harris, Pete Aguereberry, Seldom Seen Slim, and many others added character to what would one day become a national park.

There are a variety of other drives, some of which should be approached with caution. A few years back we attempted to explore a backcountry road near Ubehebe Crater—the one that would pass Teakettle Junction and conclude (for us) at the Racetrack. We'd successfully made the drive before, but on this particular trip the road became a jungle of rock after about 10 miles; it would have taken us hours to reach our destination. No one else was traveling the road, and we were unprepared to stay overnight should we break down. We turned around, knowing there were many other drives.

Years of exploring here have taught us how to optimize our seasonal selections, and you may want to review our suggestions. But keep in mind that we're not trying to diminish the adventure of spontaneity, the lure of the unknown, or your constitutional right to make and learn from your own mistakes. This isn't a blueprint and never could be, for the experiences of one will always be different from those of another.

The West Side Road is a 40-mile-long dirt road (often rough) that takes you to the area historians believe the early forty-niners once traveled trying to escape Death Valley. The Bennett-Arcan Party had trudged through endless expanses of sand, sunk in salt marshes, ground their way over lifeless gullies of rocks and boulders, and then ascended the Panamints. Upon reaching the pass (probably Wingate Pass), someone (and there is no documentation whether that person was man or woman)—recalling their near encounters with starvation—looked back and muttered, "Goodbye, Death Valley." Though only one person from the forty-niners group had died down below, the name stuck. Today the park offers a backpacking route that might duplicate that of the forty-niners. It also offers dozens of other exciting routes; we've tried to help you decide which may be best for you.

Perhaps one of the park's most intriguing areas to visit is Scotty's Castle, named for consummate conman Walter Scott. Stories of his exploits fill volumes. "Death Valley Scotty" made money in a variety of ways, including work as a trick rider for Buffalo Bill Cody. Learning of gold strikes in California, he journeyed to Death Valley. Scotty found his riches here, not because he was a good miner but because he could spin a good yarn. Eventually this ability produced one of California's most luxurious turn-of-the-twentieth century mansions. But how did all this come about? Quite simply, Scotty was the quintessential con artist. He befriended Albert Johnson, an accident-weakened Chicago millionaire who overlooked his beguiling ways. Instead, Johnson thanked Scotty for restoring his vigor by investing his wealth in Scotty's ideas.

Scotty's story should be explored in depth, but in brief the man was Johnson's storyteller, relating fascinating stories that endeared him to both Johnson and the local populace. Review our write-up before making this trip so that you'll be able to ask better questions of one of the ranger/naturalists conducting castle tours.

Dante's View, Zabriskie Point, Ubehebe Crater, and Badwater are scenic manifestations of geology and of the erosional forces produced by regional climes. They are the equivalent to Scotty's Castle in that they tell grandiose stories, but in a more natural way. They represent areas where nature, not man, has been given the material to create the bizarre. Zabriskie Point looks like a lunarscape here on earth, while Dante's View resembles a scene from Genesis as the earth began to cool. There's the story of Ubehebe Crater with its black soil, salt brush, and recent evidence of volcanic activity. And don't forget Badwater, located 282 feet below sea level. It seems that all scribes provide a rationale attempting to convince readers that Death Valley contains a spot that may just host the world's hottest temperatures. We believe Badwater to be that place and, as you'll see, have been unable to resist the temptation to convince you of the same.

All that brings us full circle—back to the Devils Golf Course, which is only a few miles from Badwater. Here we've often trudged out into the rough, hard terrain, where you should join us as we cup our hands to our ears. Listen, and sure enough, with patience, you'll hear the land perform. Focus your attention on the sounds of the earth, buzzing with the snapping, crackling, and popping. It's the sound of the land being sucked dry—and that should alert you to the fact that the air, virtually void of moisture, is also sucking *you* dry!

Enjoy, and stay with us as we explore most of the park's mysteries, providing (remember) not a blueprint for exploring but rather a plan that, hopefully, will add to your enjoyment and make you want to join countless others who have been beguiled by Death Valley. The not-so-unpleasant upshot is that you'll be joining a group now compelled to an annual odyssey of adventure, self-discovery, and just plain contentment.

# Introduction

## Location

Death Valley National Park lies on southern California's eastern border with southwestern Nevada. In fact, small portions of the park (Phinney Canyon, Grapevine Peak, part of Titus Canyon, and the detached area of Devil's Hole) lie within Nevada.

U.S. Highway 395 is west of Death Valley. From it, California Highways 178 and 190 connect with the park. From the east, U.S. Highway 95 connects with Nevada Highways 267, 374, and 373 into the park. Interstate 15 lies to the southeast of the park and connects with California Highway 127 into the park. Las Vegas is about 100 miles east of Death Valley Junction, which leads to the east-central portion of the park. Take US 95 west from Las Vegas to California State Road 373 at Amargosa Valley, and then follow CA 190 into the park.

## Getting Started

Held tight by the Panamint Range to the west and the Amargosa Range to the east, the low desert of Death Valley National Park (lying within the Mojave and Colorado Deserts Biosphere Reserve) is approximately 140 miles long, and 30 to 45 miles wide and contains 3,336,000 acres, nearly 90 percent of which is designated wilderness.

The history and natural history of this misnamed place is fascinating, and visitors of today still marvel at the ways in which the early travelers and valley dwellers managed to survive in this incredibly beautiful, desolate, parched land.

Fortunately we have modern conveniences now, and one of them—a vehicle—is essential to visiting and exploring the park. The park is huge, and getting from one place to another requires traveling great distances. Paved roads take you through the main portions of the park; an additional 243 miles of dirt/gravel, high-clearance four-by-four backcountry roads exist for driving, hiking, or camping.

The best place to begin your visit is the centrally located (on CA 190) Furnace Creek Visitor Center. Hours of operation vary but are usually 8:00 A.M. to 5:00 P.M., reopening again for the evening program. You can purchase maps and this book, of course; obtain free park handout maps and write-ups of areas; view a video on park history; and talk with rangers concerning road conditions, hikes, and backcountry travel. Ranger talks on a wide variety of park subjects are given at the visitor center several times a day and in the evenings. From November through April you can attend ranger-led walks with interpretation several times a week; these are usually well attended. You can pick up a weekly schedule for these events at the visitor center. Or visit the park Web site at www.nps.gov/deva. On the Web you can also request maps and download lots of park information.

## Geology

Properly understood, Death Valley (in this case, a segment of the much greater Death Valley National Park) is in reality a filled-in graben. The distinction is significant, for unlike a valley, which is generally created by the erosive action of rivers, a graben is created by geological activity.

A graben is a portion of the earth's crust created by the interaction of two of the earth's tectonic plates causing the earth's surface along the plate's fault line to sink. In Death Valley the graben was created rather recently in the earth's geological history. About one million years ago, this action of the tectonic plates caused mountains on either side of the valley to begin to rise. Similar activity was taking place simultaneously throughout the Great Basin formed by California and Nevada, but the spectacle of mountain and valley is most pronounced in Death Valley.

Of particular interest is the fact that the huge trough originally created by these pressures does not *appear* to represent any great sinking action, for the elevation at the surface of Death Valley at Badwater is only 282 feet below sea level. But Badwater is really not the bottom of the graben; that elevation is much, much lower. Over the millions of years since the two plates collided, the initial deep trough has been filled with sediment deposited from the eroding mountains and by a number of ancient seas and rivers. When at Badwater, you're not seeing bedrock but are seeing the accumulations of eons. The original bedrock is almost another 10,000 feet below the surface at Badwater. If all the sediment were removed, the depth of Badwater might dip to 10,282 feet below sea level. Today the end result is a valley that stretches 140 miles long and ranges from 4 to 16 miles in width. Death Valley geology is fascinating, not only for its unusual features such as the graben but also for the antiquity of its visible geology.

In addition to its faults, Death Valley's rocks provide even more interesting geological stories. Rocks here are old beyond imagination, dating back to the Precambrian era—almost 1.8 billion years ago. You can find examples of such rocks in the Black Mountains, accessed from either the Badwater area or from Furnace Creek Wash Road, which is accessed from the road to Dante's View. The detailed stories about these rocks, however, have been lost with the immense passage of time.

*Aguereberry Point, whose namesake called it "Fine View," provides a spectacular panorama of major ranges and the valley floor.*

Other rock groups have more to tell, for these rocks come from the Paleozoic era, dating back a mere 500 million years through to 225 million years ago. Marine fossils began appearing during that era and began to accumulate from seas and lakes in Death Valley as the graben began to sink further, allowing new depositions to accumulate at various layers. Wind-deposited sands accumulated during the latter portion of the Paleozoic. Rocks from this period contain much limestone and dolomite. Today you can see examples of these rocks in a number of mountain ranges, including the Funerals, Panamints, and Grapevine as well as in the rocks of Aguereberry Point.

Chronologically, the next great geological era is the Mesozoic, between 225 and 65 million years ago, the age of the dinosaurs. During these 160 million years, the Pacific plate moved east and its pressure released deep-seated molten rock, some of which crystallized in the process of cooling and became gold. Later, these rich deposits caused the rushes at the Skidoo and Harrisburg mining areas. Igneous rocks of this period include the granites found in Cottonwood Canyon. Because of the shallow sea of the period, sedimentary rocks such as shale and limestone also manifested themselves during this era. You can see them in all their glory at Marble Canyon.

The Cenozoic era began about 60 million years ago and continues to the present. This is the period that shaped Death Valley, as we know it today. This is the time when mountains were uplifted, when the valley—or graben—was created, when giant rhinoceroses, ancient camels, deer, and the tiny three-toed precursors of modern-day horses left prints that eventually became fossils. Today you can see evidence of their passing in Titus Canyon, which also provides access to Titanothere Canyon.

Of particular significance from this era is the continued activity of the tectonic plates. In fact, Death Valley is a legacy of movement of these plates. Ten million years ago the Panamints snuggled next to the Black Mountains, but they began to slip off to the west, causing the earth's crust here to become thinner and deeper and establishing the basic shape of Death Valley.

Because Death Valley provides such classic examples of faulting, you may want to see some of the evidence yourself. Look for smooth surfaces that are almost glasslike in appearance.

The Cenozoic is the era during which volcanic activity began to occur. Ten thousand years ago, molten rock breaking through the earth's thin crust came into contact with surface water. The water flashed into steam, and the sudden pressure buildup caused the earth to explode violently. One such explosion occurred 4,000 years ago, and you can see an example at Ubehebe Crater. Other, smaller cousins surround Ubehebe, but these explosions are rather recent—they're only 1,000 years old.

Much, much older volcanic evidence is contained here in Death Valley. Twenty-seven million years before the creation of Ubehebe Crater, other volcanic activity was taking place in Nevada, flinging thousands of cubic miles of ash into air. The ash blanketed the area for hundreds of miles. The typical colors at Artist's Palate come from the various minerals in that ash, typically iron, aluminum, manganese, and magnesium. Because the earth's crust is so thin here, it could burst open and disgorge ash at anytime—reminding us that nothing here in the park is static.

Though glaciation is usually associated with more northern climes, the Ice Age also influenced what is now Death Valley National Park. About three million years ago, a series of lakes formed in the area, best dramatized by Lake Manly, which covered most of Death Valley. That lake left a legacy of salt deposits as well as evidence of marine life. Concurrent with these geological eras is the never-ending process of erosion. Water running down a mountain spreads out at its bottom, creating what is known as an alluvial fan. Today we can see countless alluvial fans in the park. Though it may appear that water is scarce, it sometimes comes in torrents—and then has the power to move huge rocks. If you drive the roads here following a storm, you'll see the power of water and better understand how the many conspicuous fans radiating down the park's slopes were created and are still changing their shapes.

Nature leaves nothing static here. In the future you may well see some features that have been drastically altered from your visits in previous years.

## Sand Dunes

Park officials say that on windless days—when sands at Eureka Dunes are dry and unseen forces send columns of granules streaming down a steep bank—the friction of grain against grain can create a sound resembling bass notes played on a pipe organ. As skeptics, we've made many climbs to the top of the highest dunes in that area to listen. On several occasions we've met with less than the hoped for effects. Once the wind picked up and virtually engulfed us in a cocoon of sand. But on another occasion we heard the "singing sand."

We had departed just before sunrise on a late January day, and there wasn't a breath of air. Perhaps it was our walking that triggered the cascade, for as we watched the rapid descent of cascading sands, we heard the music and now concur that it resembles air resonating deeply in a column of pipes.

Sand dunes are phenomenal areas for many reasons. They're fascinating simply by virtue of their existence. Five areas of dunes are found in the park, and they exist because there is a source, there is wind, and there is a means of trapping the windblown sand.

In Death Valley the potential for sand is derived from the abundance of canyons and washes throughout the park. Rain, snow—and the erosional effects of freezing and thawing—create loose particles that are picked up by winds that blow at speeds greater than 10 miles per hour. Velocity is important, as this is the power required to heft the weight of the particles. Sometimes these winds blow at considerable greater speeds, and then larger amounts of sand are transported. The trick is to capture and contain these particles.

Essentially the strong winds that transport sands in Death Valley blow from two different directions. In winter the winds tend to come from the north; in summer they come from the south. When these strong winds are reduced, they drop their loads of sand particles. Winds are further reduced by landforms, which create crosswinds, rendering the winds powerless as agents of transportation.

Over the years, wind has dropped lots of sand. You can see for yourself just how much by walking between two large dunes. Often you find mudlike expanses of playa, which appears cracked and seems as though it is made from mud. In reality it represents salt deposits laid down hundreds of thousands of years ago, when vast inland seas covered the area. Though many other geological events have occurred since then, the towering dunes are a testimony to the power of wind and to some of the more recent (geologically speaking) years of deposition.

Although the creation of dunes has required thousands of years, the ripples occur on a nightly basis—any night following heavy winds. Each grain of sand is small, and winds blowing at about 10 miles per hour are strong enough to transport grains. Each grain "jumps" and then bumps other grains of sand in a process known as saltation. This jumping movement takes place at or near ground level, but the force is adequate to bump other grains until it appears as though the sands are actually flowing. Eventually the heaviest particles stop and build up several inches until there is a ripple effect that is particularly dramatic in the cross-lighting of sunrise and sunset.

Although the dunes appear to offer little that might welcome life, early morning walks reveal just how alive they can be. As you look out across the dunes, you see pockets of brush—easily identified, since only a few species can withstand the harsh conditions imposed by sand dunes. To do so, they have evolved specific structures.

Pickleweed has tiny leaves, which help minimize water loss. Generally, wherever you see pickleweed you can assume that water is not far beneath the sand's surface. Inkweed has fleshy leaves used by Native Americans as a black dye; they used the leaves and seeds for food. Natives Americans also used salt-brush, and you'll recognize the species by its flat leaves. The plant extracts salt from the sand, which sometimes results in leaves with a salt deposit on their surface.

If you visit the dunes in spring, you'll recognize the creosote bush by its yellow flowers. Later in the season, check for white balls on the plants, which house the seeds.

The largest and perhaps most conspicuous plant in the dunes is the mesquite tree, which essentially survives by producing an extensive root system that extends 50 to 60 feet down. Mesquite trees produce thorns as well as a nutritious fruit. Mesquite was important to the Shoshone Indians. In late summer the plant produces a yellow bean pod, which the Shoshone harvested for food. Branches provided wood for houses and fire, and the relatively luxuriant growth attracted various animals, some potential game.

One animal mesquite attracts is the coyote. On some days you might see a coyote slinking between mounds of sand in the early morning as the sun rises over the dunes. What's it eating? Although there may not be lots for a hungry coyote, the vegetation that pops up at various places throughout the dunes does provide a home to a select few wildlife species, evidenced by their many tracks.

Most of the tracks you see will probably be those of the kangaroo rat, one of the dunes' most fascinating creatures. Over the years I've seen several—and, my, how they can leap! Kangaroo rats are so named because of the powerful hind legs that enable them to leap long distances. You might see one if you sit quietly by a clump of mesquite late in the evening. Look for a mound of dirt containing a hole, and then sit quietly. What you're looking for is a large mouselike creature with long legs and a huge tail. When you see one, it will

*Death Valley Dunes following a sand storm, which obliterated all tracks and "freshened" the surface.*

often be hopping along on its hind legs, examining the surrounding brush for seeds. When it finds a morsel, it stores the seed in its large cheek pouches. When startled, kangaroo rats can leap long distances with surprising accuracy to a predetermined spot. The long tail helps the animal balance, and by whipping its tail it can alter its direction.

The dunes are also home to several other species, including the kit fox, several different species of lizards, the shiny black circus beetle, and the sidewinder rattlesnake. Look for curved lines in the sand about a foot long and spaced about a foot apart. The looping action of the snake creates the prints.

The Death Valley Dunes, also known as the Mesquite Flat Dunes, are located near Stovepipe Wells, easily accessed from CA 190. The park contains four other dunes sites as well, and each offers something unique. The Death Valley Dunes, for example, are crescent, linear, and star shaped.

The 10,000-year-old Eureka Dunes contain some of the tallest dunes, more than 600 feet, said to be the highest in California. Not only are they high but they host five species of endemic beetles and three species of plants found nowhere else: Eureka dune grass, Eureka evening primrose, and shining locoweed. The dunes can be accessed from two directions. From inside the park, take the road from Grapevine Ranger Station toward Ubehebe Crater, staying to the right on the dirt road at the junction with the crater road. Travel

44 miles of graded but very rough dirt road to the dunes, making sure to turn left at Crankshaft Junction (the halfway mark). An easier drive is from outside the park, departing from the town of Big Pine. (See Trip 29, Eureka Sand Dunes, for details.)

The Saline Valley Dunes are low, spreading over a large area, and are sometimes difficult to reach because of winter snows and flash floods. The route to them is the road into the remote Saline Valley, which is very long, sometimes arduous, and sometimes impassable. Saline Valley Road is north of Panamint Springs, off CA 190 or south of Eureka Dunes on a four-wheel-drive road that's for experienced drivers only.

The Panamint Dunes are the only dunes in the park that perch on a slope. They're accessible from CA 190 south of Panamint Springs, where you can see them off in the distance at the edge of the Panamint Valley, about 5 miles away. (See Trip 27, Panamint Dunes, for details.)

The Ibex Dunes are home to the Mojave fringe-toed lizard. They can be reached by traveling to Saratoga Springs in the extreme southeast corner of the park, and then hiking about 1 mile.

## The Heat Factor

When Charlie Callagan steps into his car in summer, he uses a glove or a rag to avoid burning his hand. "The handle's just too hot," says the ranger, adding that when he goes to the weather station in July and August, he often puts a wet towel around his head. "When I return to the entrance station twenty minutes later," says Callagan, "it's dry."

Coping with intense summer heat is almost a six-month project—one that transcends the individual effort. Because ground temperatures in Death Valley often approach 200 degrees Fahrenheit, water from local springs, which provide water for park service housing, gets so hot that residents turn off the heater for the hot water tank. They then reverse the spigots so that the hot water tap becomes the cold water tap and the cold water tap becomes the hot water outlet. "It's so hot," says Callagan, "that the water is hot enough to wash dishes and do anything else that requires hot water. What's interesting is that water from hot water tank, which has been sitting, is relatively cool." Staff houses are equipped with "swamp coolers," large box-like frames with fans that blow air over water-wetted plants and cool the air by about 20 degrees. Folks switch to air-conditioning when it really sizzles.

Enduring the torrid conditions unique to Death Valley has become a topic of much fascination. "Summers used to be quiet here," says Callagan, "but not any more. Now we get fifteen, twenty, twenty-five tour buses here a day. People want to experience world-class heat for themselves. 'Come on,' they say. 'Bring it on. Doesn't it get hotter than this?'"

In July an "ultramarathon" is held in Death Valley for the strong of heart. Runners go 150 miles, from Badwater to Mount Whitney, with support cars following. This is quite a feat, since even the horses are taken out of the park in the summer months.

Evaluating the weather is a big deal for Death Valley visitors. In fact, it is an event to which visitors are invited, enduring with some stoicism the awful Death Valley heat that at times has been a killer.

Death Valley may be the hottest place on Earth. Although the world air temperature record is held by Libya, which registered 136 degrees at Azizia weather station, Death Valley has an official record of 134 degrees at Furnace Creek, on July 10, 1913. "It was so hot," one observer said, "that swallows were falling dead out of the sky." But 20 miles away, Badwater averages four degrees hotter on any given day. It follows, therefore, that on that historic day in 1913 when the temperature was 134 degrees at Furnace Creek, it was 138 at Badwater. Unfortunately there was no one around at Badwater to record the event. Temperatures didn't approach those extremes again until 1998, when the mercury rose to 129 degrees. That's the hottest it has been here since that record day in 1913.

Temperatures are read from a weather station at Furnace Creek, set about 5 feet above the ground, and ground temperatures are normally 50 percent higher than in the box. Callagan calls the rain gauge there "the loneliest in the world." Summer temperatures in Death Valley average about 120 degrees, meaning that ground temperatures at the weather station are 180 degrees.

The incredible heat is the result of essentially three factors. The first is the topography. The mountains are high and narrow, trapping and holding the heat. The canyons are narrow and also trap the heat. Rather than rising and dispersing into the atmosphere, the heat sinks back into the valley. This compounds the situation, for as the air sinks it is compressed, an act that also generates heat and raises the temperature even further. The two other heat-generating factors are the lack of moisture and the lack of vegetation.

Despite the intense heat, the real concern—the potentially killer concern—is the almost complete lack of humidity in Death Valley, particularly in summer. On a typical June, July, or August day, when the temperature has risen above 120 degrees, relative humidity might be little more than 3 percent. With conditions such as these, a person can loose two gallons of water just sitting in the shade. Since blood is primarily water, the results are somewhat predictable: Circulation becomes sluggish, muscles cramp and become fatigued, the head aches, and the heart strains just to keep pumping.

A loss of three gallons of water can have even more devastating effects: Your hearing goes and your eyes sink. With a loss of four gallons, bloody cracks appear on your skin, and generally death soon follows. According to Callagan, the area now known as Death Valley has been the site of many deaths, but the summer of 1905 might have been the worst: Thirteen men died of thirst and dehydration.

Some misguided travelers have been more fortunate. Several years ago a father and son rode bicycles in May over Daylight Pass and then down toward Beatty. Their goal was to cycle the Titus Canyon Road. Someone had told them there was water at Daylight Pass, which there's not. The uphill struggle left the father severely dehydrated without the expected water at Daylight Pass. Later the father was rushed to a hospital, where he recovered.

## The Fragile Desert Soil

A "biological soil crust" covers much of the desert area, at least in places not covered by green plants. Since much of your exploring will involve walks and hikes, a mention of the extremely fragile desert soil is in order.

Soil crusts exist in both hot and cold regions, and their existence is crucial to the health of the soil. The "crust" is really a ground cover that helps reduce erosion, holds in water, and provides nutrients to the soil. Often you will see patches of hard, dark, rather bumpy "stuff," which is actually mature soil crust. The immature crust is usually the same color as the soil, almost impossible to see. Some soil crusts that you might be familiar with are lichens, mosses, and algae.

We once saw a bumper sticker that said STOP! DON'T WALK ON THE DIRT. IT'S FULL OF LIFE. Obviously, this admonition cannot always be followed to the letter. But there are many things you can do to help preserve a healthy desert, following zero-impact principles.

Footprints and tire tracks put great stress on the soil. The living crust covers only down to about ⅛ of an inch, so it is easily disturbed. Try to stay on established roads and paths, and don't create new ones. Walk on crust-free slickrock or in washes whenever possible. If ropes or signs block areas, stay clear. Desert plants are also fragile, and although they can recover more quickly than the soil crust, the damage lingers.

A reminder to "pack it out": Garbage and human waste decompose very slowly in the dry desert conditions, and burying such matter may prolong the process even more. The explorers who come after you will be grateful for your consideration, and you will have done your part to help preserve our desert environment.

## Plants of the Valley

Death Valley provides a home for some 970 species of plants, although most can be found growing in other places as well. Nineteen of those species, however, are classified as endemic to the area, meaning they are confined to Death Valley and grow nowhere else in the world. Because weather patterns are constantly changing, those numbers may increase or decrease. For example, some

*Tracks beneath a creosote bush mark one of the night's activities in Death Valley Dunes.*

plants that now grow only in higher elevations might one day grow in lower elevations, and vice versa.

Scientists have proven that much change has occurred in Death Valley and that those changes have drastically modified distribution of the park's fauna and flora. As proof, scientists point to a number of long-abandoned packrat nests.

Biologists know that packrats range no more than 70 feet from their nests. As a result, everything in the nest comes from the immediate area, including plants that today normally grow at much higher and subsequently under much cooler and wetter conditions. Carbon dating shows these plants to be about 2,400 years old, indicating that the climate of Death Valley was substantially different at the time and therefore hosted much different plants. In those days Death Valley even contained a large lake.

Today, conditions are again changing. In fact, in the past few decades the amount of annual precipitation has almost doubled—from an average of about 2 inches per year to about 4 inches. How this will affect the distribution of plants is yet to be seen, but botanists anticipate there will be change.

Despite the changes, the number of species for such an arid-appearing area remains high. Nevertheless, park ranger Charlie Callagan says that if you learn three species of plants, you'll be able to identify 90 percent of the plants you see here in Death Valley. Essentially that's because most visitors confine themselves to the more extreme areas of the park. If you range into all areas of the park, you'll find an extraordinary variation. What's important to remember is that fall and winter water conditions must be abundant and somewhat consistent for desert plants to bloom in spring. Some years yield almost no flowers at all, while others are bonanza flower years.

Perhaps the most common species found in Death Valley is the creosote bush (*Larrea tridentata*), which in January begins to produce tiny yellow flowers with five petals. Visitors walking the sand dunes near Stove Pipe Wells will see it; so will those driving the roads throughout the park's lower elevations. Creosote bush is a hardy shrub that produces a strong and recognizable creosote odor. Creosote thrives, often to the exclusion of other plants, essentially because its roots secret a poison that kills any other plant. When water is scarce, the individual creosote preserves a perimeter of open space and a monopoly on local moisture sufficient for its survival. However, when water is not so scarce, other plants sometime grow near or even under the creosote bush.

Another of the three most common plants here is the desert holly (*Atriplex hymenelytra*), interesting because the plant produces both male and female varieties. Actually, the plant is not a holly but rather a salt brush. In January the male plant is a pale green color, while the female plant is dark green. This plant produces tiny pink flowers resembling berry clusters. In the heat of summer, when the plant is dormant, its leaves become pink.

The last of the three most common species is the honey sweet (*Tidestromia oblongifolia*), a low-growing bush often found near desert holly. The leaves are fuzzy and the stems have a pinkish tinge; sheep in particular seek out this plant.

These three species are ones you can recognize almost from afar, but there are others you'll also want to learn to recognize. One quite common plant, is the arrowweed (*Pulchea sericea*), which you'll see as "corn shocks" in the Devil's Cornfield near Stovepipe Wells. In season the bush produces pink flowers. The stems are long and very straight, and the stems were indeed once used by American Indians for their arrow shafts. Arrowweed also grows along the trails leading from the upper loop at Texas Spring Campground.

Honey mesquite (*Prosopis glandulosa*) is actually a small tree with pretty fern-like leaves and a light yellow edible bean pod. You'll find these trees in areas of springs, such as Mesquite Campground.

Pickleweed (*Allenrolfea occidentalis*) not only loves water but also tolerates salt water. You'll find this pretty plant with its jointed stems growing in places like Salt Creek along CA 190, north of Furnace Creek.

In canyons and washes you'll find such common plants as sprucebush (*Peucephyllum schottii*), which produces yellow flowers, smells like pine, and has twisted branches. Rocknettle (*Eucnide urens*), also found in washes and canyons, has large, bright-green leaves—covered in bristles that you want to avoid. Its flowers are also abundant, large, and quite lovely.

In very dry washes look for turtleback (*Psathyrotes ramosissima*), a low-growing, compact plant. Producing yellow flowers, this nice-smelling plant has gray, wrinkled leaves.

Along roads and in washes you'll find the interesting Desert trumpet (*Eriogonum inflatum*), a tall plant with hollow bulges at the base of the yellow flower stalk. The leaves of this plant are round and silvery green and grow only at the base of the plant.

Many people think that deserts are overflowing with all types of cacti, but this is not so in Death Valley. Even though the Mojave Desert is rich with cacti, these and other succulent species find it nearly impossible to thrive in Death Valley. The heat, dryness, and salty soil combine to prevent many cacti species from proliferating here, and although you will find some species growing anywhere from 400 feet up to the mountaintops, none lives on the valley floor. Barrel cactus, silver cholla, and beavertail cactus are the most common. In the piñon-juniper woods, look for grizzly bear prickly pear. In all, thirteen species of cacti live in the park.

The Joshua tree (*Yucca brevifolia*), a member of the lily family, is found in abundance in the Lee Flat area. There is also a nice stand on the Big Pine Road above the Eureka Valley. From 7,000 to 9,000 there's a belt of junipers and a fair growth of piñon pines. Along the trail to Telescope Peak—at 10,000 feet—there's a stand of limber pine and a few bristlecone pines. Here in Death Valley the bristlecone pine trees, although about 2,000 years old, are not exceptionally old. That distinction goes to those found in Nevada's Great Basin National Park, where bristlecones are nearly 4,500 years old. Other parks have bristlecones as well, including Utah's Bryce Canyon—but at 500 years old, those trees are mere youngsters.

If you're interested in an American Indian experience, a favorite place to harvest piñon nuts is Hunter Mountain. In the park you can harvest them for your personal consumption but not for resale. Those in the know say that nuts baked for about thirty to forty-five minutes in an oven or heated in a pan over a fire are delicious, tasting a bit like roasted peanuts.

## Death Valley Wildlife

Mammals are the largest group of living critters in Death Valley (about fifty-one species) followed by reptiles (thirty-six), the fish (six), and finally amphibians (five). The visitor center at Furnace Creek provides lists of the park's various animals.

The mammals range in size from the tiny desert shrew, which is found near sagebrush or at the base of plants, to the desert bighorn sheep that roam Death Valley at all elevations, usually at or near a water source. At least fourteen

*Coyote stalks prey through the rocks of a wash.*

species of bats, many species of mice, several types of kangaroo rats, porcupines, skunks, foxes, mountain lions, and coyotes have adapted to this harsh land.

Death Valley reptiles include the threatened desert tortoise, the chuckwalla, many lizard species, and about seventeen species of snakes, including the Panamint rattlesnake and the Mojave Desert sidewinder. Amphibians include two species of toad, the Pacific tree frog, and the exotic (nonnative) bullfrog. Fish species include five types of pupfish and the exotic Western mosquito fish. (In the case of exotics, the park's goal is to remove them.) Five species of beetles are endemic to Death Valley, and they're all found at Eureka Dunes.

Obviously, the mammals are the easiest to search for, from their droppings to their tracks in the sand dunes. Exploring dunes can be an adventure for the entire family; this is where, if you look carefully, you'll discover much. The tracks of coyotes, foxes, lizards, kangaroo rats, jackrabbits, birds, and that infamous sidewinder can all be found at one time or another in the sand.

And—lest you think we forgot—Death Valley National Park has birds—and not just the roadrunner. Probably between 200 and 300 birds dwell in or migrate through Death Valley. Ravens, hawks, turkey vultures, herons, sparrows, hummingbirds, owls, and eagles are just a few of the varieties to be found. Because Furnace Creek Ranch has running water and greenery, it is a good place to look for birds year-round.

# Death Valley's Bighorns

Bighorn sheep are the park's largest mammal and although fascinating for many reasons, they are of particular interest here simply by virtue of their adaptive qualities. In order to survive in one of the world's driest areas, they are 10 to 15 percent smaller than their Rocky Mountain cousins. In part because of the adaptations Death Valley's bighorns have been able to make, biologists come to the park to study these mountain monarchs—one of the most social of all mammals.

One extensive study was conducted in 1956 by the team of Wells and Wells, who found that bighorn sheep can go without water for long periods. In the north, sheep can usually eat snow to replenish water losses, but not so in the desert. Here sheep frequently go days—even weeks—without water. To get by, they eat the water-holding leaves of barrel cactus, until they find free water.

Bighorn sheep, have attracted much attention through the years because of the bellicose nature exhibited by the males. In the animal world, few contests are more vigorous or is the ritual more complex than among mountain sheep.

When two rams collide, the dynamics of motion are immense. Bodies telescope. Ridges and grooves of horns tear out hair from opponents and often leave imprints. Necks twist and shock waves ripple along the animals' hide from front to rear. Often shoulders are broken and the area around the eyes torn. Horns get splintered, noses broken.

Such battles are used to determine male hierarchy during the mating season. They are an attempt to preserve the health of the species—particularly significant in Death Valley. The victorious rams mate with the ewes, and toward the end of January through mid-February lambing takes place, generally on a rocky, isolated cliff.

Lambs quickly learn from their moms where to locate some of the park's 400 springs. Sheep don't hang out at the springs, though, because this is where the predators also come. Instead they generally visit the springs in early morning or late evening.

Approximately 600 bighorn sheep make their home in Death Valley. Good places to spot them include Klare Springs and Willow Springs.

# American Indians of Death Valley

American Indians dwell year-round in the heart of Death Valley. The Timbisha Shoshone Tribe lives just south of Furnace Creek. (*Timbisha* means "red rock face paint.") Visitors are welcome to the Tribe's village, but they ask that you check in at the Tribal Office when you arrive.

The history of American Indian habitation of the Death Valley area is an ancient one. A thousand years ago the landscape here was very different from today and provided the ancient peoples with all their needs. There were springs, a variety of plants, and wildlife to hunt. Then, as today, the inhabitants harvested the abundance of nuts and beans found here, particularly the piñon pine nuts and mesquite beans. Basket weaving was an art—one that is still practiced today.

The Indians wandered this arid land according to the seasons of harvesting and hunting, enjoying their family life, religion, and mores. But when the pioneers came in the mid-1800s and mining began in Death Valley, the old way of life changed radically. No longer could the Indians count on water sources belonging to them exclusively, and the piñon trees they depended on were cut down for wood. For a period in the 1860s, the settlers and Indians waged battles. In 1866 a peace treaty was signed, the Treaty of Ruby Valley. The United States was granted right-of-way across Shoshone land, but did not gain ownership of the land.

Inevitably the Shoshone people needed to work with and follow the rules of the whites, who still came to this land in droves. They were able to obtain menial jobs to help sustain their economy but remained poor and in danger of losing much of their culture. In 1936 the Shoshone people were allowed to stay on forty acres of land inside what had become Death Valley National Monument. Very few amenities other than substandard housing units were provided.

Today the outlook is brighter. In 1983 the Timbisha Shoshone became a federally recognized tribe, and their lot in life is improving. In 2000 the Timbisha Shoshone Homeland Act transformed 300 acres of parkland to the tribe as tribal land, including the 40 acres they have been on since the 1930s. Many sacred sites lie scattered throughout Death Valley, and tribal members are working to map these out so that they will remain undisturbed. Some members work on conservation and water issues. The Shoshone still gather piñon pine nuts in fall, and that event is a special time for them—a time when many come together to celebrate their ancient culture.

# Death—And How to Avoid It in Death Valley

Over the years Death Valley has taken many lives, beginning perhaps with Val Nolan, who died, according to his epitaph, A VICTIM OF THE ELEMENTS. Since

*Val Nolan, "a victim of the elements," thought to be one of the park's first victims, probably died from heat exhaustion.*

then many others have perished or come close to it, such as the father and son described earlier who survived because of a stroke of luck.

Not all have been so fortunate. Along the highest reaches of Death Valley, up along the flanks of the slopes proceeding to Telescope Peak, hikers have slid to their death on the snowfields. Several years ago two young soldiers from Camp Irwin went exploring in their jeep and ran out of gas. They attempted to walk out of Death Valley to safety but perished. One of the soldiers was found along a dirt road where he had succumbed from dehydration and exhaustion. The body of the other was never found, although 2,000 soldiers from the base searched for a week.

According to a worker at Furnace Creek Store, 2002 was the hottest year in eighty-nine years. Like all people who have endured records, he enjoyed talking about some of the events he experienced. He said that a man died out in the sand dunes during July of that year. The man had taken water with him but not enough. When he sat down, exhausted, on the far side of the dunes, no one could see him. Soon he passed out. "When they found him," said the store operator, "his skin was so burned it had gotten black. He suffered from third-degree burns."

Death is obviously a subject of both fascination and concern in Death Valley, for many have lost their lives here, particularly in the early years of park history. The summer of 1905, the height of the Bullfrog Rush, was probably the deadliest for what is now Death Valley. That summer, thirteen men died of heat and heat exhaustion.

Each week during winter and early spring, naturalists offer interesting and informative talks. One such talk is "101 Ways to Die in Death Valley," a real attention-grabber. The ranger joked and said he would speak only of the most prevalent five or six ways visitors might get into trouble in the park.

Simple car rollovers are the most deadly happening in Death Valley. It's easy to drive too fast, and people are not prepared for the curves and narrow roads. Dehydration is another way to become very ill, and it can be fatal. The temperature in Death Valley in June, July, and August is often 120 degrees in the shade, and it remains hot at night. Drinking at least one gallon of water per person per day is recommended. The ranger spoke of one man who tried to walk the 6 miles across Badwater in July. Although he carried as much water as he could manage, he died ¼ mile from his car on his return trip. Under normal circumstances the man was just a five-minute walk from his car, which was even possibly in sight, but that day ground temperature at Badwater was 202 degrees.

Those in the know say not to hike alone, and the reasons should be obvious. Rangers emphasize that you should let someone know of your plans, especially if you are going into the backcountry. They caution that you should also be aware of other things, such as snakes. The sidewinder rattlesnake lives in the lower elevations; the Panamint red rattlesnake lives higher up. The latter rattle a lot; the sidewinder does not. Snakebites in Death Valley generally happen when people sit without looking or when they're clambering on rocks. And believe it or not, several people have been bitten while attempting to catch rattlers.

Tunnels are intriguing, but many mines and tunnel shafts are a major danger. Most caves and tunnels considered hazardous have DO NOT ENTER signs posted, and the warnings should be heeded. Dangers include collapse, bad air, weak wood, vermin and their droppings, and snakes. Several mines are open, and park personnel can inform you which are safe.

One last thing to bear in mind when visiting Death Valley: It's a good idea to leave your pet at home. Animals are not allowed in the wilderness or on trails and must be leashed at all times where they are allowed. The heat inside a car or trailer is too much for a confined animal. Coyotes pose a real danger to loose pets, and they are numerous—especially around campgrounds, where they are infamous for snatching cats and small dogs. We recently saw a sign that read, LAST YEAR FOUR CATS WERE EATEN BY COYOTES AT FURNACE CREEK CAMP-GROUND. DO NOT LEAVE PETS OUT AT NIGHT.

All that said, death in Death Valley is rare. Just use common sense, and you won't become "a victim of the elements."

# Map Legend

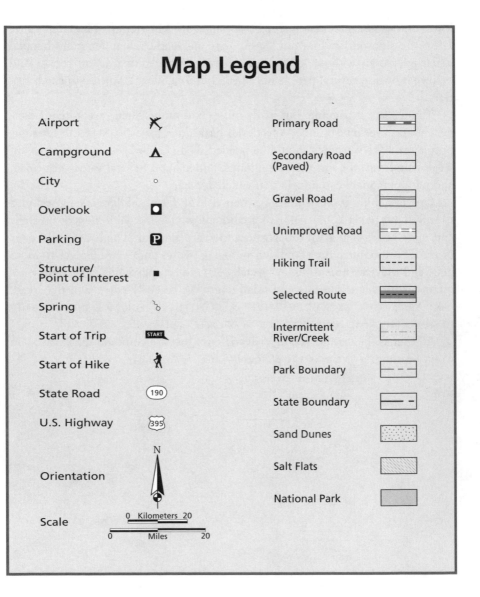

Airport

Campground

City

Overlook

Parking

Structure/
Point of Interest

Spring

Start of Trip

Start of Hike

State Road

U.S. Highway

Orientation

Scale

Primary Road

Secondary Road
(Paved)

Gravel Road

Unimproved Road

Hiking Trail

Selected Route

Intermittent
River/Creek

Park Boundary

State Boundary

Sand Dunes

Salt Flats

National Park

# Hikes and Drives North of Furnace Creek Visitor Center

## 1 - Harmony Borax Works

**TYPE OF TRIP:** Short drive and walk with optional hikes.

**DISTANCE:** 1.7-mile drive one-way from Furnace Creek.

**TYPE OF VEHICLE:** Passenger car.

**DIRECTIONS:** From Furnace Creek, drive north on California Highway 190 for 1.7 miles to the signed road and parking lot on the left (west). Follow the path from the parking lot up and around the works. *NOTE:* A separate Borax Museum is located near the entrance to the Furnace Creek Ranch and is well worth a stop. The backyard is filled with artifacts from the borax days; inside the museum you'll find gem displays and information about borax in general.

**MAPS:** Park handout map; National Geographic/Trails Illustrated Topo Map 221.

### Description

Harmony Borax Works is one of the most popular stops in the park. The works made Death Valley famous in several ways. Borax quickly became the "white gold" of Death Valley after it's discovery on the salt pan of the desert floor in 1881. There are several old borax sites in the valley area, but Harmony was perhaps the most famous. Using twenty-mule teams, miners transported borax to distant markets. From Harmony Works, the mules pulled the loaded wagons (sometimes weighing as much as thirty-six tons), 165 miles to the train depot in Mojave. It's a testimonial to the builders of the huge wagons that some of the original ones are still intact. In the 1950s and 1960s, the television series *Death Valley Days* (hosted one season by a movie actor named Ronald Reagan) romanticized the mineral, the historic period, and the people who worked the claims to extract the borax. Anyone over age thirty-five can probably remember seeing the mule teams on television, advertising "20-Mule Team Borax," which sponsored the show.

Borax made some lucky people millionaires almost overnight. In the peak years of the late 1800s, several mines existed in the area. By the end of the era in the late 1920s, some $30,000,000 worth of borax had been taken from the

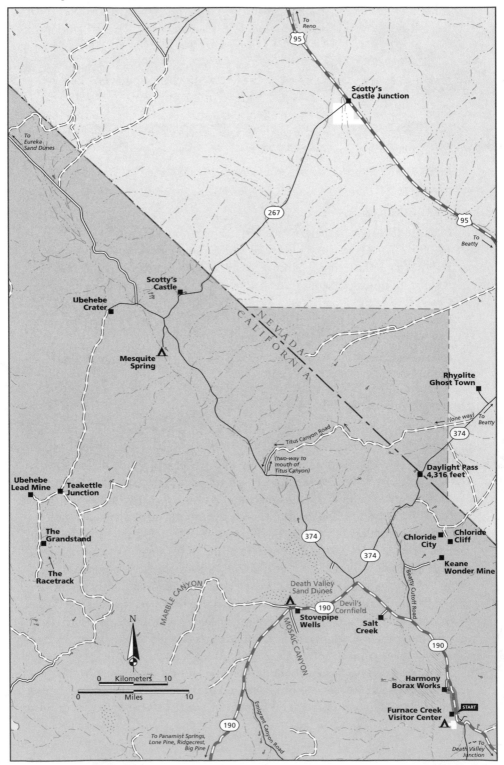

Death Valley area. Although some borax was mined here until the 1970s, today only the Billie Mine remains operational. It lies just outside the park border on the way to Dante's View. Harmony Borax Works was active for only five years, from 1883 to 1888.

Although other substances have replaced some uses it once claimed, borax is still utilized today in many ways. Because it dissolves easily in water, borax (sodium tetraborate) makes an excellent detergent, disinfectant, and water softener. When used in strong doses, borax can be used as a weed killer. Paradoxically, farmers sometimes use it as a fertilizer. Because of its fibrous nature, borax is still used as an insulator. When combined with glass, ceramics, and enamel, it lowers their melting temperature.

Although the record is somewhat obscure, the romanticized version of the discovery of borax in Death Valley drifts back to 1881 and focuses on Aaron Winters. The test for borax involved lighting crystals upon which alcohol and sulphuric acid had been poured. If the substance burned green, then it was borax. Sitting in his cabin, Aaron lit a match, touched it to the chunk of white mineral in his hand, and watched as it burned. Turning to his wife he said the magic words: "She burns green, Rosie. She burns green."

*Large teams of mules and horses once pulled huge wagons loaded with borax to trains for shipment.*

After the discovery of borax in the area, subsequent chapters in the mineral's history saw the 1880s ushering in hundreds of Chinese laborers, whose camp spread over the desert. Here they spent their days chopping up and gathering the borax clusters (which look like crystals) and then hauling wagonloads to the huge vats to be refined through several processes into pure borax. Despite the high value of borax, the works did shut down in the intense heat of summer—which meant that the workers had to toil all the more diligently when it was cool.

Some of the mineral's history is retold at Harmony, where you can view one of the old wagons used to haul borax to distant railway centers. Harmony also preserves vats in which the mineral was boiled. As you make the loop walk around the works, look eastward and try to imagine the tent city set up to house the workers. You can also make a 5-mile (round-trip) hike out to the salt flats, which should add to your appreciation of the hardships endured by the Chinese laborers. This trail goes west off the Harmony Trail.

Before leaving Harmony Borax Works, you can take a short (0.4-mile) drive through Mustard Canyon by turning left on a one-way dirt road (before you leave the parking lot), which brings you back to CA 190. If the day is hot, you'll wonder how the men, mules, and equipment endured. The walls of the canyon (mustard, of course, in color) are made of mud and salt minerals and do little to inspire a sense of well-being, which would have been folly. Harmony Borax Works preserves well the feeling of the past and another small aspect of Death Valley's remarkable history.

**TYPE OF TRIP:** Walk.

**DIRECTIONS:** From Furnace Creek, drive north on California Highway 190 for 15.1 miles to the signed turnoff on your left (west). A 2.4-mile gravel road will take you to the large parking area for Salt Creek.

**MAPS:** Park handout map; National Geographic/Trails Illustrated Topo Map 221.

## Description

It's a warm February day and we're moving quietly along the boardwalk at Salt Creek. Suddenly the water is alive with movement—a school of tiny fish about 1.5 to 2 inches long is darting through the water.

The fish are desert pupfish, a tiny fish we have come to respect because of its hardiness and their habitat. One day several years ago, I had seen these fish on a hot May day when evaporation had almost depleted the waters of this creek. Today, however, in early February Salt Creek is flowing with some authority, providing some clues to a much larger picture.

Even with the increased winter flow, Salt Creek has no visible connection with water systems outside Death Valley. The waters here at Salt Creek are insulated from the world and have been for a very long time. That it once connected

*Salt Creek is home to the rare desert pupfish.*

# Salt Creek Nature Trail

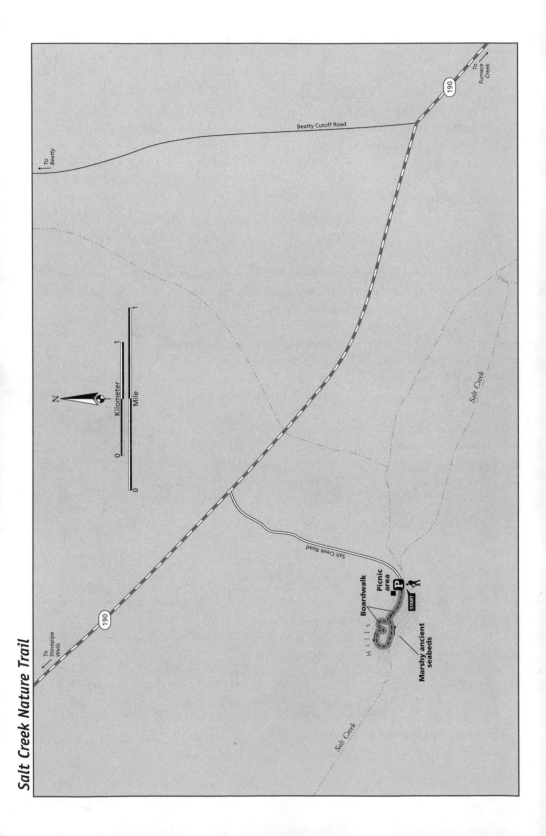

with the outside world, there can be no doubt. Because pupfish are also found in some of the larger rivers systems surrounding Death Valley, geologists know that Salt Creek once tied in with these waterways. But what's happened since those times? The pupfish has adapted well to Salt Creek's inhospitable conditions. Place another type of fish here, and the heat and salinity would wipe it out.

These adaptations did not take place overnight. About 20,000 years ago large populations of pupfish inhabited huge freshwater lakes in this area, including Lake Manly, which then covered Death Valley. (There is ample evidence of ancient shorelines 600 feet above Badwater). Lake Manly was connected with other water systems, including the Mojave and Amargosa Rivers. North America was covered with glaciers, but when those of the Sierra Nevada Mountains began to melt, they created a connection with Lake Manly. At times these waters also connected with the Colorado River, creating a route for desert pupfish. Today all of these areas still have pupfish, but none has *Cyprinodon salinus*. In fact, the fish you see here at Salt Creek are found nowhere else in the world.

In order to survive here, pupfish need several specialized organs. Because salt in the creek may slightly exceed ocean salinity, these pupfish have an organ similar to that found in ocean fish to filter out salt. They also must be able to tolerate the hot temperatures (100 degrees plus) of summer—by burrowing into the mud. Some pupfish still die when the creek begins to dry. Some select the wrong channel or pool and suffocate when it completely dries up.

Spring is the best time to see desert pupfish, and it is particularly exciting to see them as they are spawning. Stand quietly and observe the bright blue males as they defend their territories, chasing other males.

Spawning begins in February and continues through summer in the deep pools. Pupfish reach maturity in several months, and though their average life span is six to nine months, some may live several years. They feed on bugs and algae and can be cannibalistic. Those that don't live out their biological potential generally perish from predation or because summer heat has depleted their water source.

Pupfish are well adapted to the unique conditions of Death Valley. They hold in their tiny bodies the answer to the mystery of adaptation. In the past, they were so abundant that local American Indian tribes harvested them with nets. Although the fish are tiny, when collected in large numbers and then baked, they are said to be delicious. But now this largesse goes to the great blue heron, the raven, and the killdeer.

As you walk along the 0.5-mile boardwalk, you'll see other features that are indicative of highly specialized conditions. Pickleweed, the plant that seems so highly segmented, would not do well in extremely dry desert conditions, but it does do well in soil that is extremely salty, for like the pupfish, it also has a filtration system designed to reduce salt. So does salt grass, which differs from pickleweed in that its leaves are long and lancelike.

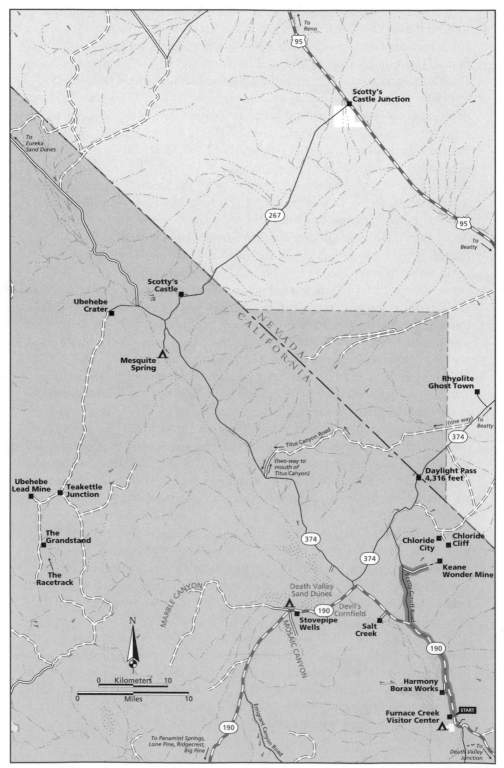

# 3 - Keane Wonder Mine

**TYPE OF TRIP:** In-and-out drive on dirt/gravel road from paved road.

**DISTANCE:** 19.1 miles one-way from Furnace Creek.

**TYPE OF VEHICLE:** Passenger car.

**DIRECTIONS:** From Furnace Creek, travel 12 miles north on California Highway 190 to the Beatty Cutoff Road (signed). Go 5 miles to the sign on the right (east) for Keane Wonder Mine. Drive 2.9 miles on the good dirt road to the parking area at the base of the Funeral Mountains.

**MAPS:** Park handout map; National Geographic/Trails Illustrated Topographic Map 221.

## Description

The first thing you'll note about this site is how high up on the cliffside this construction is—the mill you see before you is nearly a mile lower than the actual mine. An obvious trail leads past the mill and goes about 1 mile up to the mine. The photo opportunities here are quite good, not only of the valley but also of the mill, artifacts, and mine. You can poke around here as you wish—do walk the worn trails around the sides of the mill.

Jack Keane discovered very high quality gold and silver here in 1903. Four years were spent constructing the mill and the tramway, and the latter was an outstanding engineering feat. The tram was almost a mile long, held up by eleven wooden towers. Buckets bearing ore were carried by gravity and cables for 1 mile down from the mine, with a vertical drop of 1,300 feet. Then the gold, silver, and lead were hauled to the town of Rhyolite, Nevada, at least 15 miles northeast.

The mine played out in 1916, but not before it paid out about $750,000. Mines in Death Valley are an integral, fascinating part of its history. Exploring these out-of-the way places makes one realize the depth of the determined, rugged, adventurous, sometimes desperate souls who once toiled in this harsh land.

*Keane Wonder Mine.*

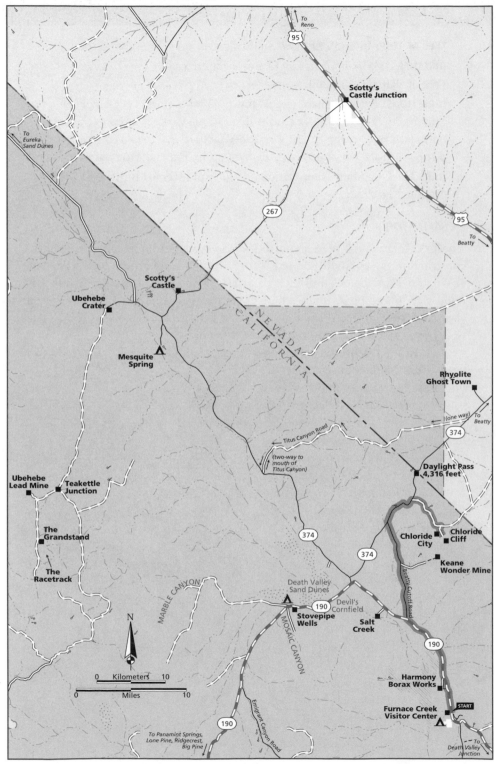

To Reno
95
Scotty's
Castle Junction
95
To Beatty
To Eureka
Sand Dunes
267
Scotty's
Castle
Ubehebe
Crater
NEVADA
CALIFORNIA
Mesquite
Spring
Rhyolite
Ghost Town
(one way) To
Beatty
374
Titus Canyon Road
(two-way to
mouth of
Titus Canyon)
Daylight Pass
4,316 feet
Ubehebe
Lead Mine
Teakettle
Junction
374
374
Chloride
City
Chloride
Cliff
The
Grandstand
Keane
Wonder Mine
The
Racetrack
MARBLE CANYON
Death Valley
Sand Dunes
Devil's
Cornfield
190
Stovepipe
Wells
Salt
Creek
N
MOSAIC CANYON
190
0    Kilometers    10
0    Miles    10
Harmony
Borax Works
Furnace Creek
Visitor Center
START
To Panamint Springs,
Lone Pine, Ridgecrest,
Big Pine
Emigrant Canyon Road
190
To
Death Valley
Junction

**TYPE OF TRIP:** In-and-out, backcountry drive.

**DISTANCE:** Approximately 33 miles one-way from Furnace Creek.

**TYPE OF VEHICLE:** High-clearance, four-wheel drive recommended; no trailers.

**DIRECTIONS:** From Furnace Creek, drive north on California Highway 190. Take Beatty Cutoff Road (signed) and go over Daylight Pass toward Beatty, Nevada. Turn south onto a rough dirt road just prior to the NEVADA STATE LINE sign. Go 7 miles and turn right. After 4 more miles, turn left and travel a couple more miles to the site of Chloride City. To reach Chloride Cliff, continue south on the dirt road for about 0.5 mile.

**MAPS:** Park handout map; National Geographic/Trails Illustrated Topo Map 221.

## Description

If you are in the mood for a rather rough road trip to an interesting area with spectacular views, this one is for you.

The mining ruins and the Chloride City area offer some of the oldest remains in the park, dating back to 1871, when silver ore was discovered here. Chloride City was not begun until 1905 and was peopled by those working the mines. The town didn't endure for long, it became a ghost town in 1906. The mines opened and closed many times over the next three decades, finally shutting down for good in 1941.

The wooden structures have collapsed, but remains of some stamp mills can be seen. Any artifacts, be they rusty cans or rotted wood, should not be disturbed.

If you continue to Chloride Cliff, you'll be treated to a wonderful panorama of Death Valley. According to one ranger, Chloride Cliff once was in hot contention with Dante's View as the number-one viewing area in the park. Dante's View won out.

For the more adventurous, there is a cross-country route between Chloride Cliff and the Keane Wonder Mine, which lies below. Talk with a ranger about this trip, and purchase a topo map of the area before attempting it.

# 5 - Titus Canyon

**TYPE OF TRIP:** A backcountry drive that begins in Nevada, 2 miles east of the park boundary, and concludes at the canyon mouth about 11 miles north of the Stovepipe Wells junction in Death Valley. *NOTE:* This one-way road is sometimes closed to vehicular traffic in summer; check with rangers prior to your trip. Trailers are not allowed at any time. Plan on at least half a day or longer.

**DISTANCE:** Approximately 55 miles total to the end of Titus Canyon in Death Valley; 27 miles are on a dirt road, all one-way except for the last 2.5 miles out to the paved road. Begin this trip from Stovepipe Wells, traveling 21 miles on paved road to the access of Titus Canyon, 6 miles southwest of Beatty, Nevada.

**TYPE OF VEHICLE:** Titus Canyon road is graded periodically. We drove a four-wheel-drive truck, but some visitors used passenger cars with decent clearance. Drivers should be comfortable with very narrow, twisty roads and steep drop-offs. Since this road is subject to flash flooding, it is best to check with rangers as to weather forecasts and current conditions.

**DIRECTIONS:** From Stovepipe Wells, take California Highway 190 northwest for 9 miles to the junction with Scotty's Castle Road. Go left and almost immediately take your first right, State Road 374, toward Beatty, Nevada. You'll travel through Mud Canyon and reach Hell's Gate and then cross Daylight Pass (elevation 4,316 feet) before you begin to drop down to the Amargosa Desert Valley. Shortly after leaving the park boundary, you will come to the signed Titus Canyon Road on the left (west).

**MAPS:** Park handout map; National Geographic/Trails Illustrated Topo Map 221.

## Description

The drive through Titus Canyon, albeit a bit rough, is one of the most popular trips in the park, and justifiably so. The trip offers glimpses of unique geological formations, petroglyphs, and springs frequented by mountain sheep and from one vantage point provides views of controversial Yucca Mountain. Stops along the way provide insights into the area's mining history as well as access to some great hikes. The drive, however, is not for the faint of heart. The road winds over narrow roads with steep drop-offs, and toward the end proceeds through tight-walled canyons.

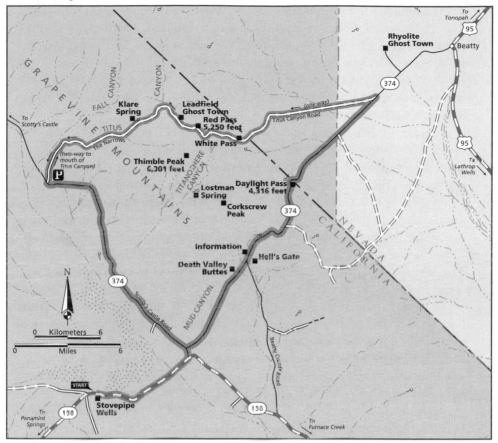

The road is one-way for cars, but hikers can go against the traffic and access the canyon 12 miles north of the junction of Scotty's Castle Road and CA 190 or 18 miles south of Grapevine Ranger Station. Be on the lookout, though, for cars coming through the canyon.

The drive begins in the Amargosa Valley and quickly ascends the Grapevine Mountains. It then enters Titanothere Canyon, where the remains of dinosaurs have been found and where you may well see sheep, particularly if you take the time to hike down and into the canyon to one of their favorite watering areas. Although there's no marked trail you can access the drainage by stopping at the second fork in the drainage and then walking down about 4 miles, a route that will take you to Lostman Spring.

Continue your drive—as you must, for there's no turning around—to the 5,250-foot elevation and incredibly spectacular crossing of Red Pass. From here the road drops quickly to the abandoned mining site of Leadfield. You'll want to park your vehicle and explore the now-abandoned mining town and perhaps dwell on its short but colorful past.

As with other mining towns in Death Valley, Leadfield got its start through misrepresentation. Built as a result of wild and distorted advertising, the town was established when 300 hopeful miners swarmed to the area about August 1926. Six months later the post office closed and the town died. All that remains are two buildings and several massive piles of dirt that represent the miners' efforts. A series of unofficial short trails lead to the buildings and offer what may be a much-needed leg stretcher.

Despite the lack of mining success, the area looks as though it should be loaded with minerals. All around are twisted and distorted rock, evidence of the ages. A close look at some of the rocks will reveal the presence of ancient marine life— the fossils of various types of shells. Because similar organisms are found today only in vast seas, it's not a stretch of the imagination to say that seas must once have covered this area. Add a bit of mountain building, and then twist those mountains with mighty geological forces and you have today's landscape. Before you are sands and silts compressed and hardened into limestone. The lesson is one of time, and the time span required to alter the area from ocean to mountains was 500 million years.

Leaving Leadfield you begin driving through the main fork of Titus Canyon. Limestone cliffs surround the wide wash, formed by running water many years ago as the Grapevine Mountains were tilted upward. You're now at Mile 16.3 and next to a mountain that exhibits some of the park's most dramatic examples of folding. Here the layered mountain looks like pancakes stacked one on top of the other—and then tilted upward at a 45-degree angle.

Approximately 2 miles from Leadfield is a sign for petroglyphs on the right. In certain light they are difficult to see; they have also been defaced by thoughtless visitors. Here, too, is the site of Klare Spring, evidenced by the abundance of greenery. Take a moment or two to walk among the luxuriant growth and you might see matted areas where sheep have paused to rest. You might also see their tracks in the mud. The springs are one of the few areas in the park where desert bighorns are seen on a consistent basis.

From Klare Spring, continue your drive and prepare for more geological spectacles. From about this point, you'll see examples of the Titus Canyon anticline, part of which is associated with Corkscrew Peak, visible at Mile 19.7. Between Miles 20 and 23, watch for ripple marks and more rock foldings. Look, too, for limestone beds that have been shattered. It's all highly dramatic and evokes that sense of "Wow! What happened here?"

At Mile 23 the road enters a step-walled canyon that threads for 1.5 miles and is the final part of the trip. As you drive, take time to appreciate the power of water, which has cut your route through these walls. All too soon the dirt road breaks out onto a large alluvial fan that signifies the end of your Titus Canyon tour. From here it is about a mile drive onto the two-way dirt road and CA 374.

**TYPE OF TRIP:** Drive and walk.

**DISTANCE:** 35 miles northeast of Furnace Creek or 4 miles west of Beatty, Nevada, on Nevada Highway 374.

**TYPE OF VEHICLE:** Passenger car.

**DIRECTIONS:** From Furnace Creek, take California Highway 190 north for 12 miles to the signed Beatty Cutoff on your right. Go 10 miles to a T intersection at Hells Gate (there is a visitor kiosk). Turn right (northeast) and follow California Highway 374 toward Beatty, Nevada, crossing over Daylight Pass. Go about 16 miles and turn left onto on a paved road to Bull Frog Mine and the town of Rhyolite (signed). Or from Beatty travel southwest on NV 374 for 4 miles to the right-hand turn into Rhyolite.

**MAPS:** Park handout map; National Geographic/Trails Illustrated Topo Map 221.

## Description

According to park statistics, the average visitor to Death Valley remains 1.5 days. When we visited Clint and Ellen Boehringer in 2003, we learned they had been exploring Death Valley, and specifically Rhyolite, for the past eleven years. To save money they have been doing so as volunteers for the Bureau of Land Management, leaving their home in Oregon and parking their camper for about seven months each year on a spot overlooking the now-abandoned town of Rhyolite. Although Rhyolite is just outside the park near Beatty Nevada, we include it here because the history of Rhyolite is so closely linked with that of Death Valley.

Rhyolite contains the remains of many buildings. Only two are still intact, and one of these may be one of the most unique structures anywhere. It's Tom Kelly's bottle house and, as the name implies, is built entirely from bottles.

Tom Kelly began his bottle house back in 1905 when he was seventy-six years old. He had a wealth of sources to choose from—the relatively small town of almost 8,000 residents relied on some fifty-three saloons for their spirits. Beer, wine, and hard liquor came in sturdy glass bottles, and the bottle house reveals their strength. Most of the bottles used once held Adolphus Busch beer, which later became Budweiser. Clint says that Kelly used almost 30,000 bottles and that there's probably close to that many still intact—and if you don't believe him, you can count them.

Because Rhyolite was nearly abandoned by 1910, the town fell into disrepair, and so did the bottle house. But in 1920 Paramount Studios came to town,

# Rhyolite Ghost Town

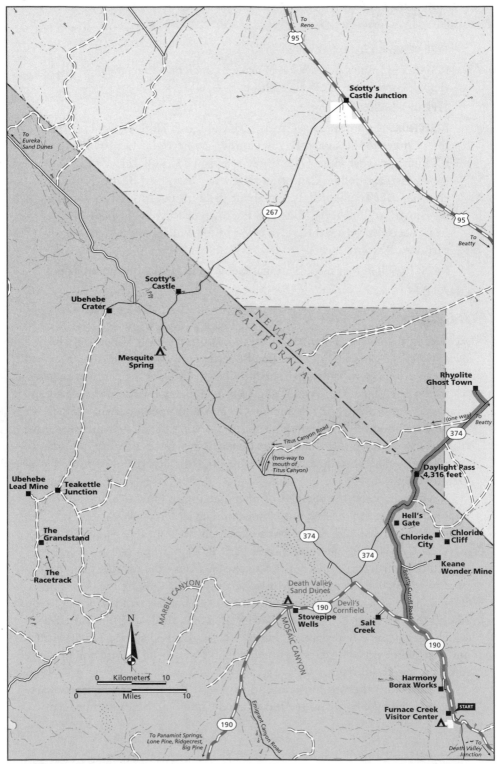

To Reno

95

Scotty's
Castle Junction

To
Eureka
Sand Dunes

267

95

To
Beatty

NEVADA
CALIFORNIA

Scotty's
Castle

Ubehebe
Crater

Mesquite
Spring

Rhyolite
Ghost Town

(one way) To
Beatty

374

Titus Canyon Road

(two-way to
mouth of
Titus Canyon)

Daylight Pass
4,316 feet

Ubehebe
Lead Mine

Teakettle
Junction

374

Hell's
Gate

Chloride
City

Chloride
Cliff

The
Grandstand

Keane
Wonder Mine

The
Racetrack

MARBLE CANYON

374

N

Death Valley
Sand Dunes

Devil's
Cornfield

190

Stovepipe
Wells

Salt
Creek

Beatty Cutoff Road

0    Kilometers    10

0      Miles      10

MOSAIC CANYON

190

Harmony
Borax Works

Emigrant Canyon Road

Furnace Creek
Visitor Center

START

190

To Panamint Springs,
Lone Pine, Ridgecrest,
Big Pine

To
Death Valley
Junction

fixed up the house, and used it in a movie. Tommy Thompson took over management in 1954 and was the last to manage the house, doing so until 1989. He and his wife, Mary, operated the house as a curio shop. They also interpreted the town so that visitors would understand Rhyolite's somewhat wild and woolly days.

Rhyolite got its start in the same way as other Death Valley mining towns: word of mouth—in this case from a man whose name is closely linked with Death Valley, Shorty Harris, although to some extent from Ed Cross as well. Apparently, Shorty drank a little too much of the "Ol Be Joyful," and when he traveled in and around Death Valley, he also talked too much.

In 1904 Harris and Cross were prospecting in the area and found quartz all over the hill. "The quartz was just full of free gold," declared Harris. "This district is going to be the banner camp of Nevada." Before long, men had staked over 2,000 claims, the most promising being the Montgomery Shoshone mine, which prompted a mass move to Rhyolite.

Rhyolite grew quickly and before long included a variety of social activities, ranging from basket making and baseball to opera and school picnics. In 1907 Rhyolite got electricity. That same year, mines were producing as much as 300 tons of ore a day, and several miners claimed they could generate $10,000 in a single day.

*Clint Boehringer has been explaining Rhyolite's unique features for several years, including the 30,000-bottle bottle house.*

Although 1907 was a banner year for Rhyolite, it was also a year of financial panic. The panic took its toll, and by 1910 the newspaper had closed, mill production was down to $246,661, and only about 600 residents remained. By 1916 the town had lost its powerhouse and lighthouse and the railroad had ceased to run.

As noted earlier, today only two complete buildings remain: the train depot, which is privately owned, and Tom Kelley's old bottle house. When you visit, be sure to ask for the witty and informative booklet *Rebecca's Walk Through Time* by Suzy McCoy.

# 7 - Scotty's Castle

**TYPE OF TRIP:** Drive and walk.

**DISTANCE:** 54 miles one-way from Furnace Creek or 45 miles one-way from Stovepipe Wells.

**TYPE OF VEHICLE:** Passenger car.

**DIRECTIONS:** From Furnace Creek, go north on California Highway 190 for 18 miles to the junction (north) with Scotty's Castle Road (California Highway 374). Travel 33 miles to the north turnoff (signed) to the castle, just past Grapevine Ranger Station. It's 3 miles up Grapevine Canyon to the castle and parking lot on your left. From Stovepipe Wells, go north on CA 190 for 9 miles to the intersection with Scotty's Castle Road, and follow directions above.

**MAPS:** Park handout map; National Geographic/Trails Illustrated Topo Map 221.

## Description

A castle in Death Valley? Although the impetus for its existence may not be the world's greatest scam, it certainly rates near the top. This castle in the desert should be one of your must-see Death Valley stops.

Creation of the castle goes back to 1904, when miner/cowboy/con artist/teller of tall tales Walter E. Scott convinced Chicago millionaire Albert Johnson to grubstake him in his efforts to extract more gold from a mine he claimed had already produced gold. Scotty indeed had gold to show Johnson. What Scotty *didn't* say was that the gold he presented had actually come from his wife, who had obtained it in Colorado as a souvenir. The nuggets persuaded Johnson that he should grubstake Scotty. But rather than embarking on a bona fide search for gold, Scotty squandered the grubstake in Nevada and California.

Johnson was a good businessman, however, and wanted to evaluate the mine for himself.

Johnson arrived in Death Valley and toured the desert with Scotty, listening and enjoying the tall tales that Scotty told him. More important, Johnson's health, which had suffered immensely following a railroad accident, began to improve. Johnson, no fool, soon realized that there was no mine, but he was so grateful for the restoration of his health that he forgave Scotty. And so began a lifelong friendship that soon resulted in the beginning of "Scotty's" castle.

The foundation began in 1915 when Johnson began purchasing sizable plots of about 1,500 acres in Grapevine Canyon, located in what is now the northeastern portion of Death Valley. The land contained good springs, which you can still see today.

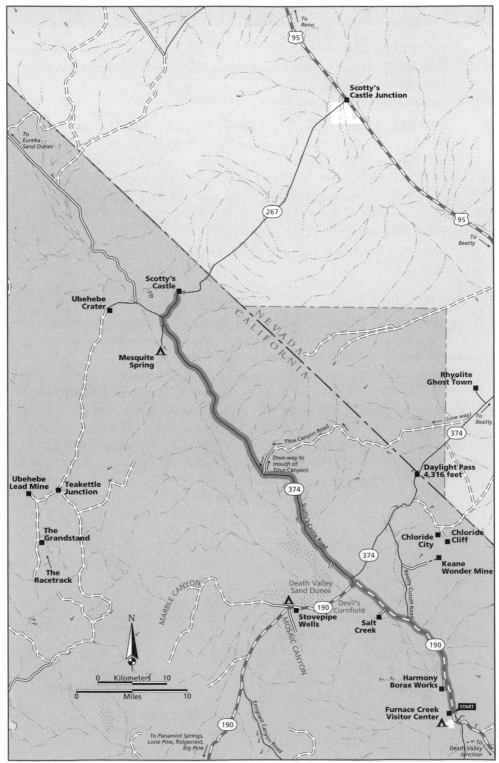

To Reno
95
Scotty's
Castle Junction
To Eureka
Sand Dunes
267
95
To
Beatty
Scotty's
Castle
Ubehebe
Crater
NEVADA
CALIFORNIA
Mesquite
Spring
Rhyolite
Ghost Town
(one way)
To
Beatty
Titus Canyon Road
374
(two-way to
mouth of
Titus Canyon)
Daylight Pass
4,316 feet
Ubehebe
Lead Mine
Teakettle
Junction
374
Scotty's Castle Road
Chloride
City
Chloride
Cliff
The
Grandstand
374
Keane
Wonder Mine
The
Racetrack
MARBLE CANYON
Death Valley
Sand Dunes
Devil's
Cornfield
190
Beatty Cutoff Road
N
MOSAIC CANYON
Stovepipe
Wells
Salt
Creek
190
0    Kilometers    10
0         Miles         10
Harmony
Borax Works
190
Furnace Creek
Visitor Center
START
Emigrant Canyon Road
190
To Panamint Springs,
Lone Pine, Ridgecrest,
Big Pine
To
Death Valley
Junction

About the same time, Johnson began bringing his wife, Bessie, to the land. At first they lived in large tents, but eventually Mrs. Johnson convinced her husband that they should build a ranch. Over the next nine years, Johnson poured almost $1.5 million into the home, contracting with a railroad company to import materials.

Johnson, owner of an insurance company in Chicago, allowed Scotty to live in his developing home while he was away on business. As a result the home soon began to acquire the personality not only of the Johnsons but also of Scotty.

Scotty's Castle really is a castle, built in the Spanish Provincial style and sprawling over many acres. Originally the place consisted of a main structure and servants' quarters and measured 32 by 96 feet. Then the Johnsons began a more castlelike construction, and the result reflects their incredible attention to detail. The castle has turrets, a sundial, and a 260-foot swimming pool, all of which you can see on your tour. Inside the castle there are Indian baskets, tiles, candelabra, pottery, various configurations of wrought iron, and valuable rugs imported from Majorca. The park has preserved all these treasures.

The outside is no less intriguing, and trails take you to some of the more interesting features. Adjacent to the castle is the Tie Canyon Trail, named for the 120,000 railroad ties Johnson had hauled into the valley from just north of Beatty, Nevada. The ties cost $1,500, and many still lie stacked along the path. Transporting and stacking them took several months, at an additional cost of more than $25,000. Why did he want the ties? The closest wood was in the form of piñon pines, which produce little usable wood and those trees were high in the Panamint Mountains. It was a far better deal to buy the ties for firewood, as winters can be cold at an elevation of about 3,000 feet.

Although Johnson was a shrewd businessman, he almost lost his home when he learned that it had been constructed on government land— land that was soon slated to become part of the new Death Valley National Monument. Johnson persuaded Nevada congressman Samuel Arentz to introduce a bill into the House of Representatives that would enable him to buy the land, but Pres. Franklin D. Roosevelt vetoed it. Roosevelt insisted that although Johnson could purchase the land, the government should have the first rights to buy it back. In 1970 the land become available, and the National Park Service purchased all rights.

The park provides interpretation for the site, which is carried out by persons in period costumes who are dedicated to preserving the legacy of Albert Johnson and Walter Scott—and the stories. Once, according to the interpreter, a rattlesnake came in to cool off. Mrs. Johnson had a rattlesnake figurine placed on a shelf in the kitchen to serve as a reminder to keep the doors closed.

Another story explains why a door ornament contains two holes. According to Scotty, the device optimized the capabilities of a shotgun loaded with buckshot. If *two* thieves tried to enter, only one shot would be necessary. The buckshot

*Scotty's Castle.*

would hit the metal "splitter" in the device and be deflected in two directions, simultaneously sending both assailants to Boot Hill.

To better appreciate Scotty's creative imagination, you need to see the "splitter" for yourself and hear some of the others tales the man so easily created. Many are told daily on tours the park offers year-round.

Although Scotty's Castle appears to be a completed structure, park staff says it really never had a beginning and, likewise, will never have an ending. The castle never had a beginning because it was never intended to be a castle. It never had an ending because Johnson stopped building when he discovered he was not on property he legally owned. The only true ending is one provided by the demise of Death Valley Scotty, a fitting conclusion to your exploration of the grounds.

Outside, a trail takes hikers on a short stroll to the top of a hill commanding a spectacular view of the castle and the surrounding area. Appropriately, this is Scotty's last resting place. The marker was dedicated November 12, 1954, by the Death Valley '49ers and looks out over the castle and over the land Scotty knew so well. The epitaph provides his name and his life span, 1872–1954, and further provides his philosophy of life:

> I GOT FOUR THINGS TO LIVE BY. DON'T SAY NOTHING THAT WILL HURT ANYBODY. DON'T GIVE ADVICE—NOBODY WILL TAKE IT ANYWAY. DON'T COMPLAIN. DON'T EXPLAIN.

Perhaps this quintessential scam artist had more philosophical depth than might at first appear to have been the case. Visit the castle and decide for yourself.

# 8 - Ubehebe Crater

**TYPE OF TRIP:** Out-and-back drive with optional hikes to the bottom of the crater and walks around the crater rims.

**DISTANCE:** 55 miles northwest of Furnace Creek or 43 miles northwest of Stovepipe Wells.

**TYPE OF VEHICLE:** Passenger car.

**DIRECTIONS:** From Furnace Creek, go 19 miles north on California Highway 190 to the intersection of California Highway 374 to Beatty, Nevada (east), and Stovepipe Wells (west). Stay straight (north, following signs for Scotty's Castle) for 33 miles to Grapevine Ranger Station. Just past the station, go left (west) for 5 miles to Ubehebe Crater.

**MAPS:** Park handout map; National Geographic/Trails Illustrated Topo Map 221.

## Description

At 3,000 years of age, Ubehebe Crater is the one of the most recent of a series of "marr volcanoes" to have occurred in the land now comprising Death Valley. Marr volcanoes occur when magma rising from the depths suddenly comes into contact with groundwater. The sudden contact creates a flash of steam, which then expands. When the pressure on the surrounding rocks becomes too great, they explode. In this case they created Ubehebe and Little Hebe as well as a number of other, smaller volcanoes in the immediate area. They also created a number of lesser craters in Death Valley, located to the south.

Ubehebe is located about 8 miles from Scotty's Castle or about 5 miles from Mesquite Springs Campground, one of the park's most delightful places to pitch a tent or park a camper. It is a lovely, quiet place surrounded by the Last Chance and Grapevine Mountains and sitting above Death Valley Wash, a series of rocks and mud deposited by heavy water flows. It is also adjacent to the site of marr-type volcanic activity, specifically Little Hebe and Ubehebe Craters.

There is some confusion as to the origin of the name, Ubehebe, but the most accepted is from the Death Valley Shoshone Indian word *Tem-pin-tta-Wo'sah*, meaning Coyote's Basket or Basket in the Rock. As you gaze down the 600 feet to the bottom of the largest crater, it's easy to visualize a huge colorful basket, for the eastern side in particular is filled with layers of colors.

Standing on the thick crater rim, you can pick out the many trails leading to the bottom. On the crater's east side are deeply eroded gullies from runoff. Evidence of an old lake lies on Ubehebe's floor. Early morning and late afternoon are the best times for photos and generally the best time to hike.

# Ubehebe Crater

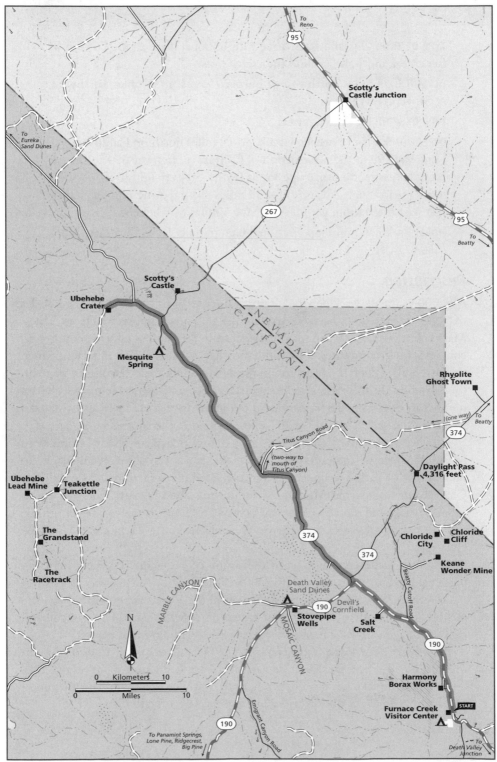

To Reno
95

Scotty's
Castle Junction

267

95

To
Beatty

To
Eureka
Sand Dunes

Scotty's
Castle

Ubehebe
Crater

Mesquite
Spring

NEVADA
CALIFORNIA

Rhyolite
Ghost Town

(one way)
To
Beatty
374

Titus Canyon Road

(two-way to
mouth of
Titus Canyon)

Daylight Pass
4,316 feet

Ubehebe
Lead Mine

Teakettle
Junction

The
Grandstand

374

374

Chloride
City

Chloride
Cliff

Keane
Wonder Mine

The
Racetrack

MARBLE CANYON

Death Valley
Sand Dunes

Devil's
Cornfield

190

Stovepipe
Wells

Salt
Creek

Beatty Cutoff Road

N

MOSAIC CANYON

190

Harmony
Borax Works

0    Kilometers    10

0        Miles        10

Furnace Creek
Visitor Center

START

To
Death Valley
Junction

190

Emigrant Canyon Road

To Panamint Springs,
Lone Pine, Ridgecrest,
Big Pine

*Even at the bottom of Ubehebe Crater, mesquite flourishes along with other species. The climb back up is a challenge.*

As park literature says, "getting to the bottom is easy; the trip back up can be exhausting." Pick a cooler day to descend, carry plenty of water, and hike slowly. You will be amazed to find that even at the bottom of the crater, there is much plant life, particularly the park's ubiquitous mesquite plant.

If a hike to the crater's often-torrid bottom is one you want to defer to another time, consider other area trails. From the parking lot at Ubehebe Crater, walk west (to your right as you're looking down on the crater) on the obvious trail to view Little Hebe Crater. From this vantage point you can easily see the 1.5-mile trail that circles the rim of Ubehebe, a fairly easy and beautiful hike. As you walk you can also see the coalescing of a number of alluvial fans—but of a special type. These are fanglomerates, which consist of sandstone and conglomerate rocks that have been cemented together by calcite.

Over the years, we've not only descended the crater numerous times but also walked it's periphery. Sometimes we've had perfectly ideal weather conditions; other times, winds have sprung up without much warning. Once the winds blew so hard it was a struggle not to be pushed one way or another by the powerful gusts created in part by the crater's depths. At times the winds can blow yet harder. Drivers are cautioned to make use of their vehicle's handbrake. There are documented cases where the winds have shoved one car into another.

**TYPE OF TRIP:** An in-and-out backcountry drive, mostly on rough dirt roads. Plan on most of a day; you'll need about three hours round-trip driving time from Ubehebe Crater. Take food, water, and a camera—and be sure to have plenty of gas. An optional hike to Ubehebe Peak is 6 miles round-trip and strenuous. The Racetrack Valley area is closed to camping.

**DISTANCE:** 83 miles one-way from Furnace Creek, 74 miles one-way from Stovepipe Wells, or 32 miles one-way from Grapevine Ranger Station.

**TYPE OF VEHICLE:** High-clearance vehicles are recommended, and you may need four-wheel drive if rain occurs. Don't even think about taking a trailer!

**DIRECTIONS:** From Furnace Creek, travel north for 18 miles on California Highway 190 to Scotty's Castle Road (California Highway 374). Take Scotty's Castle Road for 38 miles to Ubehebe Crater. The road to the Racetrack is signed at the crater road (and goes south) and now becomes dirt. In 20 miles you will reach Teakettle Junction. Continue for 5 miles to reach the Grandstand and another 2 miles to the Racetrack.

**MAPS:** Park handout map; National Geographic/Trails Illustrated Topo Map 221

## Description

Rocks that move? Twenty-five years ago, when we first heard about the phenomenon, we puzzled and puzzled. It was something we had to see, but getting out to the Racetrack can sometimes be a formidable task. The road can be washed out and badly rutted. In fact, the first time we attempted to visit this area, the road was so extraordinarily bad that we turned back, learning from the aftermath of a horrendous rainstorm just how quickly the roads can become jumbled. Of course, there are some good times to visit the Racetrack; it all depends on staffing and other park road priorities. If you can coordinate your trip to this area so that it follows a bit of road smoothing, you and your vehicle (preferably one with good clearance) will probably be much happier.

As with all backcountry road trips in Death Valley, plan this one carefully. In fact, plan as though you were going to have two flat tires, that the day would be scorching and the night frigid, and that you would be stranded overnight. Include in the scenario the thought that you would be where there's no help available and that you might not see anyone for a twenty-four hours. But go anyway—these are simply precautions to ensure your survival in the worst-case

# *The Racetrack and Grandstand*

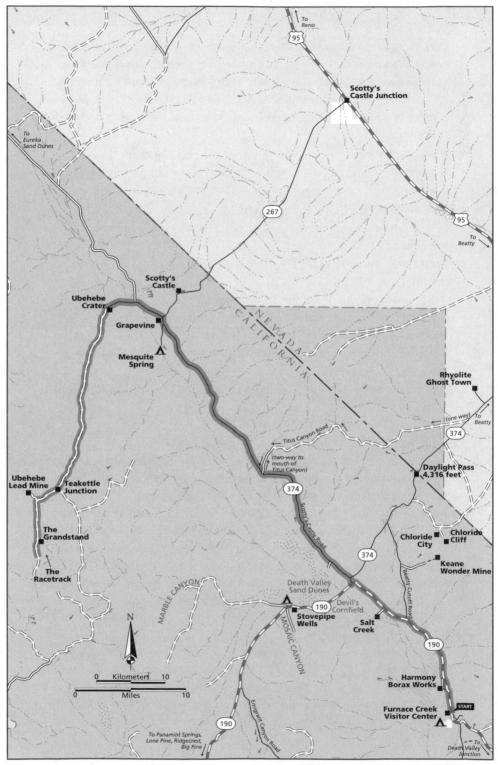

To Reno
95

Scotty's
Castle Junction

To Eureka
Sand Dunes

267

95

To Beatty

Scotty's
Castle

Ubehebe
Crater

Grapevine

NEVADA
CALIFORNIA

Mesquite
Spring

Rhyolite
Ghost Town

Titus Canyon Road

(two-way to
mouth of
Titus Canyon)

(one way)    To Beatty

374

Ubehebe
Lead Mine

Teakettle
Junction

374

Daylight Pass
4,316 feet

Scotty's Castle Road

The
Grandstand

374

Chloride
City

Chloride
Cliff

Keane
Wonder Mine

The
Racetrack

Beatty Cutoff Road

MARBLE CANYON

Death Valley
Sand Dunes

Devil's
Cornfield

190

Stovepipe
Wells

Salt
Creek

190

MOSAIC CANYON

N

Harmony
Borax Works

0    Kilometers    10

0    Miles    10

Furnace Creek
Visitor Center

START

To Panamint Springs,
Lone Pine, Ridgecrest,
Big Pine

190

Emigrant Canyon Road

To
Death Valley
Junction

scenario. We've never had a problem, and sometimes we've made the drive in an older vehicle.

The dirt-road part of the drive to the Racetrack begins at Ubehebe Crater and climbs for about 9 miles. The road takes you past a delightful forest of Joshua trees, so named by the Mormons, who envisioned the branches as the arms of a prophet raised in supplication. Suggestions of the forest remain with you for several miles, but eventually the road begins to descend and you lose the trees. Along the way you'll also see lots of creosote bushes and several kinds of cacti, including cholla, beavertail, and cotton top.

Twenty miles into your trip on the dirt portion, you arrive at Teakettle Junction, a spot where you'll want to stop and take some photographs. Over the years, visitors have hung all sizes and colors of teapots on the signpost, and it has become a colorful and fun site. (***Photographic note:*** Although you might well see the junction when it's stabbed with harsh sunlight, you'll want to use a flash to reduce hard shadows. If your flash allows you to back off a third or two-thirds of an f-stop, you can fill in the shadows created by the sun without completely eliminating them.)

Continue your drive, passing a spur road on the right 2 miles later. About a mile long, the rutted Ubehebe Lead Mine Road leads to the ruins of a lead mine that operated during the late 1800s.

Approximately 4 miles later you'll come to the Grandstand, a huge dark island of quartzite at the north end of the Racetrack. You can park here and walk 0.75 mile out to the rock. The trailhead to 5,678-foot Ubehebe Peak is west of the Grandstand parking area. It's a 6-mile round-trip hike, rated as strenuous, with an elevation gain of 1,800 feet.

In another 2 miles you'll arrive at the Racetrack, the name given to the dry lakebed known as playa. There is a campground nearby and a parking area. Motorists must park here. Do not take vehicles over the playa, which is fragile and could be altered, destroying some of the phenomenal features associated with the Racetrack.

The lakebed is about 3 miles long and 2 miles wide, and this mud layer is about 1,000 feet thick. The lakebed derives its name from the rocks that seem to "race" across the playa, sometimes over total distances that can exceed 1,500 feet.

The overriding question, of course, is how do the rocks, which tumbled from the nearby mountains due to erosion, perform this feat? How have the rocks come to rest where you now see them? Sometimes you'll see long tracks trailing the rocks like a gigantic tail, suggesting that they slid across the mud. If that's the case, what made them slide?

Although Death Valley is noted for its dryness, the answer to the mystery lies in the occasionally heavy winter and spring rains—rains so heavy that when

*Teakettle Junction.*

accompanied by winds of 50 miles per hour or more provide a slick surface over which the gusts might literally blow these rocks along. No one has ever observed the rocks moving, but this is the scenario depicted by most scientists. The rocks must have moved on many sequential occasions. Look at the marks and the distances, which suggest that rocks move little more than 20 feet during a given storm. The fact that some rocks repose in the middle of the tracks suggests that they must have traveled on many occasions. If you could only be here on one of these nights and could see the rocks "race" across the Racetrack, you could claim a first.

If you continue 2 miles south and then west from the Racetrack, you'll reach Saline Valley Access Road, an unmaintained dirt road. This is one of the roughest and most challenging roads in Death Valley and is for experienced four-wheel drivers *only*! Most visitors turn back after exploring the Racetrack.

## 10 - Zabriskie Point

**TYPE OF TRIP:** An out-and-back drive on paved roads with a short walk to the overlook.

**DISTANCE:** 4.8 miles one-way from Furnace Creek Visitor Center.

**TYPE OF VEHICLE:** Passenger car.

**DIRECTIONS:** From Furnace Creek Visitor Center, turn south (right) onto California Highway 190. After 1.3 miles, the Badwater Road goes to the right; do not turn here. Stay on CA 190 for 3.5 more miles to the signed turnoff on your right for the Zabriske Point parking lot. A short trail leads to the overlook.

**MAPS:** Park handout map; National Geographic/Trails Illustrated Topo Map 221.

## Description

Zabriskie Point is one of the most popular places in Death Valley. The soft mud, sand, and gravel deposits found here have created an incredible display of badland formations. Iron minerals contribute to the yellows, tans, and browns; volcanic ash and lava contribute to the variations of green and dark gray. Light, of course, figures into the equation, creating a parade of tonal changes during the day.

For photographers Zabriskie Point may be one of the area's most intriguing landscape formations. It's little wonder that the site has been used as a backdrop for several movie and TV creations. Can't you see Darth Vader and Luke Sky-walker moving through this land when the light is low and the hills begin to look like a multilayered cake with a fudge topping? You also can move through the land, for Zabriskie Point is a jumping-off point for hikes to Golden Canyon and Gower Gulch. Should you embark on one of these hikes, make sure you know where you're going and that you have an ample supply of water. This area recently claimed the life of a man who elected to explore the area without sufficient water in the heat of a summer's day.

Zabriskie Point, like so many other areas in Death Valley, was created over long periods from sedimentation left by the various seas that once covered the area. Before you are bands of varying colors—layered into interesting features

# *Zabriskie Point*

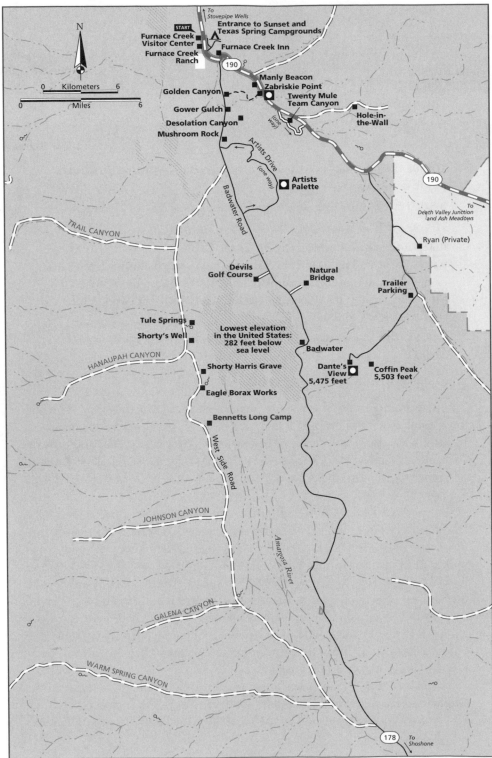

N

Kilometers 0 — 6

Miles 0 — 6

To Stovepipe Wells

START
Furnace Creek Visitor Center
Furnace Creek Ranch

Entrance to Sunset and Texas Spring Campgrounds

Furnace Creek Inn

190

Manly Beacon
Zabriskie Point
Twenty Mule Team Canyon

Golden Canyon

Hole-in-the-Wall

Gower Gulch

Desolation Canyon

Mushroom Rock

Artists Drive (one way)

Artists Palette

190

To Death Valley Junction and Ash Meadows

TRAIL CANYON

Badwater Road

Ryan (Private)

Devils Golf Course

Natural Bridge

Trailer Parking

Tule Springs
Shorty's Well

HANAUPAH CANYON

Lowest elevation in the United States: 282 feet below sea level

Badwater

Dante's View 5,475 feet

Coffin Peak 5,503 feet

Shorty Harris Grave

Eagle Borax Works

Bennetts Long Camp

West Side Road

JOHNSON CANYON

Amargosa River

GALENA CANYON

WARM SPRING CANYON

178

To Shoshone

by subsequent erosion, the handiwork of the ages. It requires but little imagination at Zabriskie Point to see the action of wind, rain, sleet, and hail transforming an uplifted area into a maze of broken ripples.

Many millions of years ago, ancient mammals such as mastodons and camels left their tracks here as they wandered through. These tracks have enabled geologists to date when these rocks were formed. The climate was wetter then, but Death Valley is in a constant state of flux. Even today, as the valley sinks, ancient rocks come to the surface.

From the overlook at Zabriskie Point, look northwest about a quarter mile. The highest peak within this landform is Manly Beacon, named for William Manly, who was in Death Valley in the mid 1800s. Following a grueling hike, Manly and his companion, Rogers, helped save the lives of pioneers who were stranded here. This feature, as well as many others in the park, commemorates his heroic journey

*Golden Canyon, one of the park's more colorful canyons, links with Zabriskie Point.*

# Twenty Mule Team Canyon

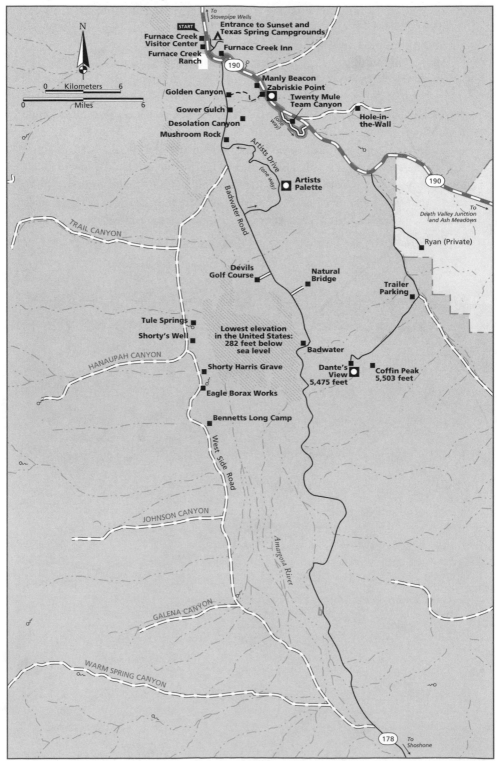

**TYPE OF TRIP:** A one-way drive on a narrow, normally good dirt road. *No trailers.* **NOTE:** This road may be closed during and after rainfall.

**DISTANCE:** Approximately 18 miles round-trip from Furnace Creek Visitor Center. Plan to spend at least a half hour to an hour on this trip.

**TYPE OF VEHICLE:** Passenger car.

**DIRECTIONS:** From Furnace Creek Visitor Center, take California Highway 190 southeast for 6.3 miles to the signed right-hand turn to Twenty Mule Team Canyon (just south of Zabriskie Point). The one-way dirt road rejoins the highway in 2.7 miles.

**MAPS:** Park handout map; National Geographic/Trails Illustrated Topo Map 221.

## Description

The canyons of Death Valley are always impressive, but this particular drive is one of the most scenic in the park, especially if the light is right. Early morning or late afternoon light enhances the vast array of colors and the badland formations inherent to the area. You actually can see this scene from Zabriskie Point, but driving into the canyon gets you "up close and personal." Like Zabriskie Point and Golden Canyon, Twenty Mule Team Canyon was created by lakes older than Lake Manly, the last of whose waters disappeared about 10,000 years ago.

You won't see many desert plants in here. For one thing, the soil is very alkaline, too salty for most plants. And erosion occurs constantly in the muddy environment, making it difficult for plant roots to grab anchor. But the alkaline soil does produce one "crop." Along the road you'll see mining tunnels burrowed into the hills by borax prospectors. Some of the borax here was high grade enough to entice miners.

Despite the valley's name, borax was never transported through the area by the twenty-mule teams. It was only mined here by people who also built the first of Death Valley's frame houses. Shortly after the area was declared a national monument, the bunkhouse/office was moved to Furnace Creek, where it now serves as the Borax Museum.

Because of its muddy nature, the road closes following a rainstorm. Be glad, for mud from rain-soaked roads builds up in wheel wells. It also can build up on wheels, throwing off a tire's balance. Of course, it seldom rains here in the park, so the road is generally available, offering some of the best views for a drive requiring so little an expenditure of time.

# Hole-in-the-Wall

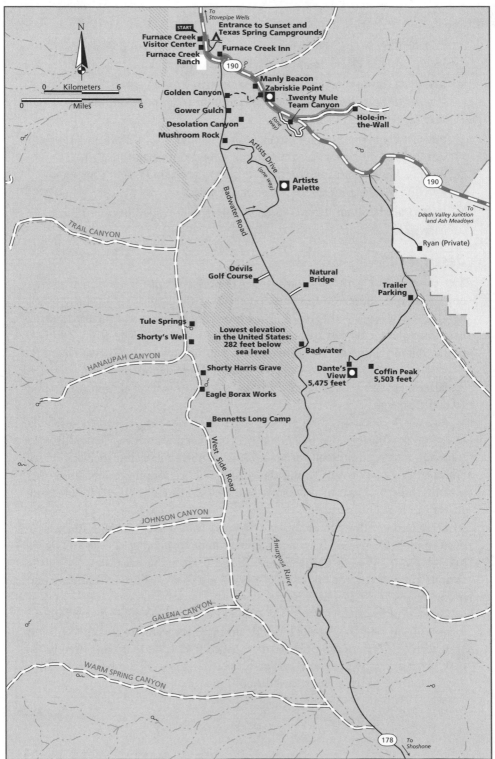

N

0 — Kilometers — 6

0 — Miles — 6

To Stovepipe Wells

START

Furnace Creek Visitor Center

Furnace Creek Ranch

Furnace Creek Inn

Entrance to Sunset and Texas Spring Campgrounds

190

Manly Beacon

Zabriskie Point

Golden Canyon

Twenty Mule Team Canyon

Hole-in-the-Wall

Gower Gulch

Desolation Canyon

Mushroom Rock

Artists Drive (one way)

(one way)

Artists Palette

TRAIL CANYON

Badwater Road

190

To Death Valley Junction and Ash Meadows

Ryan (Private)

Devils Golf Course

Natural Bridge

Trailer Parking

Tule Springs

Shorty's Well

HANAUPAH CANYON

Lowest elevation in the United States: 282 feet below sea level

Badwater

Shorty Harris Grave

Dante's View 5,475 feet

Coffin Peak 5,503 feet

Eagle Borax Works

Bennetts Long Camp

West Side Road

JOHNSON CANYON

Amargosa River

GALENA CANYON

WARM SPRING CANYON

178

To Shoshone

# 12 - Hole-in-the-Wall

**TYPE OF TRIP:** An in-and-out backcountry drive on a rough dirt road.

**DISTANCE:** 4 miles to Hole-in-the-Wall; an additional 2 miles to the end of the dirt road. From Furnace Creek Visitor Center, it is about 7 miles to the turnoff, making this a 22- to 24-mile round-trip.

**TYPE OF VEHICLE:** A high-clearance vehicle to Hole-in-the-Wall; four-wheel drive beyond.

**DIRECTIONS:** From Furnace Creek Visitor Center, take California Highway 190 south for about 7 miles to the signed turnoff to the east (just beyond the west turnoff to Twenty Mule Team Canyon). Travel on this road is not recommended during rain or when the roadway is wet.

**MAPS:** Park handout map; National Geographic/Trails Illustrated Topo Map 221.

## Description

On our scale of 1 to 10 for backcountry road conditions, with 1 being the best, we rate conditions here a 5. Scenery and interesting features, however, would rate much higher.

*Mud drips, a geological oddity seen in several Death Valley areas, are abundant at Hole-in-the-Wall, near Furnace Creek Ranch.*

The road begins not far from Twenty Mule Team Canyon and begins as a gravel wash, which heads east into the Funeral Mountains. There is some vegetation along the wash, such as desert holly. The drive is fun but requires attention because of scattered boulders. Soon the gullies give way to higher hills of conglomerate. Water has caused the interesting erosion patterns.

At Mile 4 you'll suddenly go through a huge gap, which is about 400 feet high. This is Hole-in-the-Wall, and you'll quickly see it is not much of a hole at all. On the other side of the gap you come to a faint V in the road. Stay left and park there—and then explore. If you take the right fork, the road becomes quite a bit rougher and ends in 2 miles.

Depending on your interests, you'll probably want to devote about an hour here. If you're a photographer, you may need more time, as the hills and fascinating walls make for interesting photographic studies. Mud drips have created beautiful patterns, and barrel cactus glows pink among the desert rocks in season.

The return trip offers spectacular views of the Zabriskie Point badlands, with Telescope Peak far in the background. Huge boulders make a nice foreground for photographs. You also get a peek at the northern end of Artists Drive formations. Try to pick a sunny day for this one—the colors can be exquisite.

*NOTE:* This route is a favorite of mountain bike riders, who enjoy this 8-mile, mostly flat hike/bike/drive.

**TYPE OF TRIP:** A paved road drive to the most scenic viewpoint in Death Valley, with optional hikes.

**DISTANCE:** 26.6 miles one-way from Furnace Creek Visitor Center, with two short optional hikes leaving from the parking lot. Plan to linger.

**TYPE OF VEHICLE:** Passenger car.

**DIRECTIONS:** From Furnace Creek Visitor Center, take California Highway 190 southeast for 11.9 miles to the signed right turn (southwest) onto Dante's View Road. Follow the narrow, windy road for 13.2 miles up (the last 0.5 mile is quite steep) to the parking lot at the viewpoint.

**MAPS:** Park handout map; National Geographic/Trails Illustrated Topo Map 221.

## Description

Gorgeous, incredible, superb, amazing—wow! These are just some of the adjectives we've overheard being used to describe Dante's View. This spot of beauty has one of those names associated with death or evil that occur frequently throughout Death Valley National Park. In this case, we find it a misnomer. What explorers do gain from here is a real sense of the park's immensity and diversity.

The elevation at the viewpoint is 5,475 feet; directly below is Badwater, at 280 feet below sea level. The shimmering salt flats below (also called playa) spread north and south for miles. The distance across the flats is about 6 miles. By gazing straight across the flats, you view the mighty, often snow-covered Telescope Peak (11,049 feet). Next to this giant lie Wildrose and Tucki Mountains, whose alluvial fans (caused by rock, gravel, and sand washing out of the mountain canyons) are among the largest in the park. Aguereberry Point, Trail Canyon, and miles of the Panamint Range are in view. According to the park interpretive sign, THE PANAMINTS ARE A GOOD EXAMPLE OF GREAT BASIN FORMATIONS.

Once, perhaps 12,000 years ago, what is now called Badwater was enormous Lake Manly—90 to 100 miles long and more than 600 feet deep. That was a period of ice fields and snow and constant water flows into what is now dry desert. Conditions have changed, of course, and today you can appreciate a number of vegetative zones from Dante's View. Looking across toward Telescope Peak, you'll see a band of green just below the life-giving snow with its associated meltwaters. The greenery represents piñon pine and juniper. Below that—along the middle portions of the Panamints—the vegetation dwarfs and is represented by plants requiring less moisture, such as the black brush, Mormon tea, and sagebrush. This is also the zone you are standing in at the viewpoint.

# Dante's View

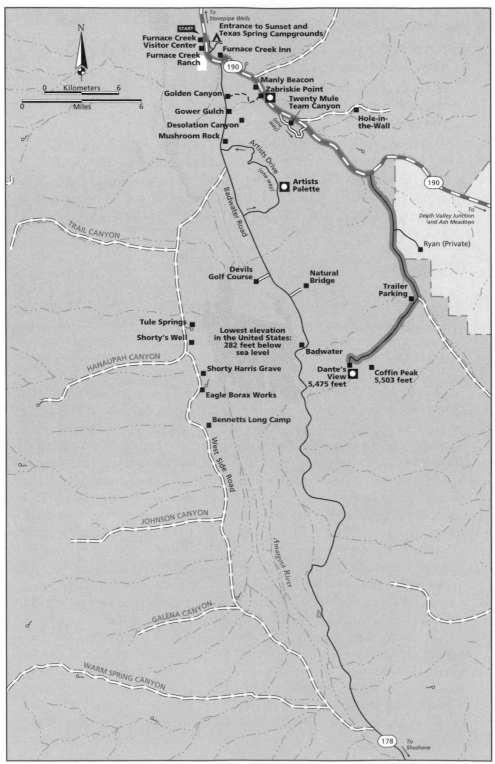

N

0    Kilometers    6

0    Miles    6

To
Stovepipe Wells

START
Furnace Creek
Visitor Center

Entrance to Sunset and
Texas Spring Campgrounds

Furnace Creek
Ranch

Furnace Creek Inn

190

Golden Canyon

Manly Beacon
Zabriskie Point
Twenty Mule
Team Canyon

Gower Gulch

Hole-in-
the-Wall

Desolation Canyon

Mushroom Rock

(one way)

Artists Drive
(one way)

Badwater Road

Artists
Palette

190

To
Death Valley Junction
and Ash Meadows

TRAIL CANYON

Ryan (Private)

Devils
Golf Course

Natural
Bridge

Trailer
Parking

Tule Springs

Shorty's Well

HANAUPAH CANYON

Lowest elevation
in the United States:
282 feet below
sea level

Badwater

Shorty Harris Grave

Dante's
View
5,475 feet

Coffin Peak
5,503 feet

Eagle Borax Works

Bennetts Long Camp

West Side Road

JOHNSON CANYON

Amargosa River

GALENA CANYON

WARM SPRING CANYON

178

To
Shoshone

Yet farther down slope, available moisture further diminishes. Only plants with long or spreading roots can exist here, such as creosote brush.

Continuing downhill and into an area of even less moisture, you find mesquite and then pickleweed. And then, finally is the "chemical desert," where life without shelter and water would soon be desiccated. Because Dante's View is somewhat removed from these harsh conditions, it is a good place to reflect on them. It is also a good place from which to strike out and explore that middle zone of black brush, Mormon tea, and sagebrush.

From the parking lot, an obvious trail heads north for 0.5 mile to Dante's Point (5,704 feet). Remember your camera for this hike, which winds around the side of the mountain. Many of the rocks are covered with bright blue, yellow, and orange lichen. The vertical relief is breathtaking, and here you get an even better impression of Badwater. Morning is the best time for photography, as the bright desert sun begins to shine on the Panamints. If you are an early riser, sunrise is the best time to be here.

Back at the parking lot, take the well-used trail south to the overlook for another impressive, slightly different view. The walk is about 0.25 mile one-way. You can sit on the rocks, sometimes a wind shelter, and take in this incredible panorama.

At any time of year, Dante's View and the surrounding area are usually windy and perhaps 15 to 25 degrees cooler than below, so be prepared with jackets and hats. Of course, if you are a summer visitor, this is the place to be to cool off.

There are no limitations on where you can explore from up here. About 0.75 mile down the road from the viewpoint is a parking area with a pit toilet. From here you can hike south (2.4 miles round-trip) up an obvious trail to Coffin Peak (5,503 feet), lying south of Dante's View. Consider it another name that, like Dante's View, might denote austere conditions that are offset by stark and inspiring beauty.

# Willow Spring

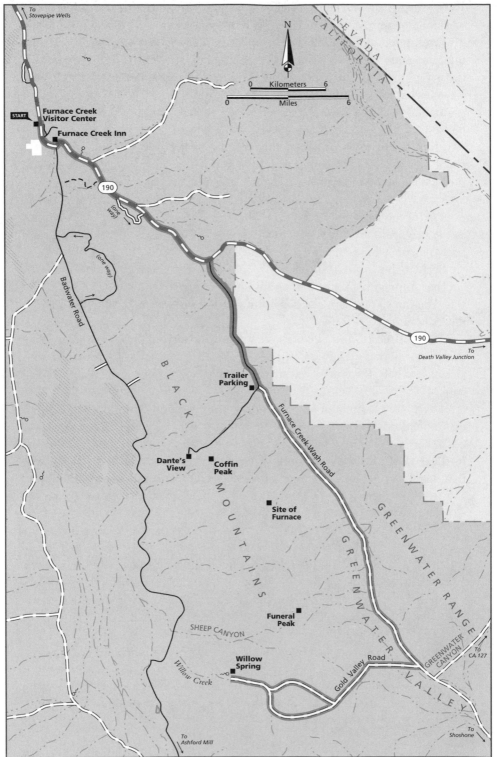

To Stovepipe Wells

NEVADA
CALIFORNIA

N

Kilometers
0          6

Miles
0          6

START
**Furnace Creek
Visitor Center**

**Furnace Creek Inn**

190

(one way)

Badwater Road

(one way)

190

To
Death Valley Junction

**Trailer
Parking**

Furnace Creek Wash Road

B
L
A
C
K

**Dante's
View**

**Coffin
Peak**

M
O
U
N
T
A
I
N
S

**Site of
Furnace**

GREENWATER RANGE

G
R
E
E
N
W
A
T
E
R

**Funeral
Peak**

V
A
L
L
E
Y

SHEEP CANYON

GREENWATER
CANYON

To
CA 127

**Willow
Spring**

Willow Creek

Gold Valley Road

To
Ashford Mill

To
Shoshone

**TYPE OF TRIP:** An out-and-back drive on mostly backcountry roads.

**DISTANCE:** 108 miles round-trip from Furnace Creek.

**TYPE OF VEHICLE:** A two-wheel-drive, high clearance vehicle is generally fine for Greenwater Valley Road; four-wheel drive is necessary for Gold Valley Road.

**DIRECTIONS:** From Furnace Creek take California Highway 190 south-east toward Zabriskie Point. Stay left on CA 190 at Furnace Creek Inn. After 26.6 miles take the right turn (signed) toward Dante's View. Go 7.7 miles to the dirt road on your left, just past a sign for trailer parking. The road is signed as FURNACE CREEK WASH ROAD and is a good dirt/gravel two-lane, especially if recently graded. Go 18.1 miles to a tall metal post on the left; here take a hard right onto a very rough, narrow dirt road. (If you count carefully on the drive in, this road [Gold Valley Road] is the fifth dirt road on the right.) Travel 13.3 miles to the road's end at Willow Spring. *NOTE:* A portion of Gold Valley Road (toward the end) is a loop. See topographic map 221.

**MAP:** National Geographic/Trails Illustrated Topo Map 221.

## Description

We left Furnace Creek Campground on a chilly morning early in February, beginning the drive to Willow Spring in search of the illusive desert bighorn sheep that often are seen in this area. As with many other Death Valley outings, getting to your destination is part of the fun.

Leaving Furnace Creek, you'll pass Zabriskie Point, Twenty Mule Team Canyon, Hole-in-the-Wall, Dante's View, Billie Mine (still in operation), and finally the settlement of Ryan, still inhabited. Billie Mine and Ryan are just outside the park boundary, but both played an important part in the history of the area. In the early 1900s Ryan was the place for early park visitors to stay.

After accessing Furnace Creek Wash Road, you travel through the Greenwater Valley, engulfed by defacto wilderness. The Greenwater Range is to the east; the dark formations to the west are the Black Mountains. Distant ranges appear, such as the Owlshead Mountains to the south. If winter moisture has been sufficient, this higher elevation valley is good for wildflower viewing in spring. Along this road are several dirt side roads (before you come to Gold Valley Road) that lead into the old mining ghost towns of Furnace and Greenwater.

After traveling about 13 miles, you'll arrive at a hard right turn, which can be confusing. You're looking for Gold Valley Road, and the sign for it is on a tall metal pole on the left. If you continue on Furnace Creek Wash Road, you'll end up in the town of Shoshone.

Gold Valley Road is quite rough; you may want to use four-wheel drive to prevent your rear tires from slipping and spinning on the loose gravel and rock. The drive is a beautiful one, passing through deep sand, rock gullies, and many washes. Meanwhile, you're engulfed by different formations, mountains, and a variety of ever-changing colors. As a bonus, the area can be extremely isolated; on the day of our trip, we saw nary another vehicle.

As you near the spring, the terrain becomes broken country, with cliffs, rocky slopes, and higher mountains. This type of area is what bighorn sheep need for their "escape terrain." Close to the road's end, we dropped into a high-walled, narrow canyon and could see sheep tracks and droppings in the sand. Looking up we saw several caves in the mountainside; in some desert habitats, such caves are often occupied by sheep during the intense heat of summer.

Abruptly, at a pile of large boulders, we were at road's end, and bighorn sheep sign was everywhere. The animals are lured by the abundant willow, sage, and reeds found at the spring. Above, growing in the rock faces, were a number of large barrel cacti. The species has great water-retention powers, and at times the succulent core can be a source of water—and food—for sheep. Surprisingly, there's no running water at the spring—but obviously it isn't far from the surface of the ground. The trees and bushes extend at least 500 yards down the canyon—probably much farther—but hiking grows increasingly difficult because of thick bushes and the steepness of the slope.

On the return trip, traveling the other side of the loop, we still averaged about 5 to 10 miles per hour. We continued our search for sheep, and although we never saw any, we knew they were there, watching us all the while.

# 15 - Golden Canyon/Gower Gulch

**TYPE OF TRIP:** Loop or in-and-out hike.

**DISTANCE:** If you hike the loop, which includes Golden Canyon and Gower Gulch, the total distance is 4 miles. Those hiking Golden Canyon only (out and back) will hike 2 miles round-trip. Another option is to hike all the way up to Zabriskie Point, for a trip of 2.5 miles one-way. For this option, you can work a shuttle with two cars—one parked at the lot of Golden Canyon, the other waiting for you at Zabriskie Point.

**DIRECTIONS:** From Furnace Creek, go south on California Highway 190 for 1.3 miles to the right-hand turn onto Badwater Road. Go 2 miles to the signed left-hand turn into the Golden Canyon parking lot.

**MAPS:** Park handout map; National Geographic/Trails Illustrated Topo Map 221.

## Description

### Golden Canyon

Death Valley preserves geological history well, and although there are many areas in the park that exhibit it in spectacular fashion, few are more accessible or more revealing for the amount of time invested than the area of Gower Gulch and Golden Canyon. But you'll need to hike, and you'll need several hours—or more. If you hike just Golden Canyon, you'll be hiking 2 miles, but there's so much to do here that you could almost spend a day in this area.

Trails from the end of Golden Canyon lead to Zabriskie Point, Manly Beacon, and Red Cathedral. Yet another trail leads to Gower Gulch—a five-hour, 4-mile round-trip hike. At about Mile 4 you'll leave the mouth of Gower Gulch, where you'll pick up a faded trail that parallels the road and returns you to the Golden Canyon parking lot, visible from the mouth of Gower Gulch. Some quick math will tell you that we've suggested a hike that mandates coverage of but 1 mile per hour. Although there are some relatively steep areas on the hike, at least for the first half, they aren't that exhausting. In fact, you could easily move along at 2, maybe even 3, miles per hour and "collect" another series of park trails. But if you rush through, you'll miss so much in an area where there's so much to see—and explore.

Golden Canyon can be accessed from several locations, but the best is from the parking lot designated for the Golden Canyon hike. Routinely, depending on staff levels, the park also offers naturalist-led hikes through both Golden Canyon and Gower Gulch. Check bulletin boards for the times and days for these interpretive hikes.

# Golden Canyon/Gower Gulch

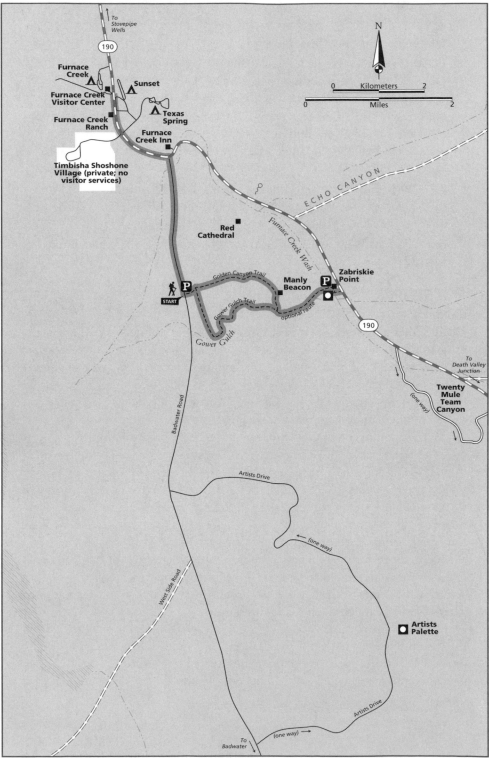

Aesthetically, Golden Canyon offers a rainbow of colors, some that stretch the imagination. It offers badland features that have been backdrops for a number of Hollywood creations. Geologically, the area offers features so ancient they seem to exceed credibility. Walk these trails and you walk through both beauty and a timeless landscape. Golden Canyon and Gower Gulch had similar beginnings to other features in Death Valley: the depositions of ancient seas. Because the Golden Canyon area is located along a fault, the land here began to be uplifted. Subsequently, occasional torrents of rain fell and flowed, creating the numerous alluvial fans seen throughout Death Valley. But here at Golden Canyon and Gower Gulch, the rains did more: They carved out several canyons—with spectacular results.

As you hike through Golden Canyon, you'll see ten numbered stakes that are keyed to an interpretive brochure detailing your immediate surroundings. Stake 1 points out that an old mining road once ran through the area and explains how a flash flood literally tore most of it out. Other markers detail such features as the alluvial fans and the type of rock you are seeing. The brochure also explains the folding and faulting that are so spectacular in the canyon and points out the abundant ripple marks, evidence of ancient Lake Manly.

The Golden Canyon hike concludes 1 mile up the canyon. You can either turn around or extend your hike. If the day is a hot one and you left late, you should turn around—the heat and lack of humidity in the area have claimed lives. If, however, the day is mild and you have the time, we suggest that you continue on. The trails wander through some of the park's most spectacular areas.

If you continue toward Zabriskie Point, you'll be treated to the beautiful Red Cathedral cliffs on the left. Then you'll be hiking under Manly Beacon, also to your left. The appropriately named Beacon juts above the surrounding landscape. Named for one of the original forty-niners, who helped bring assistance to his stranded group, Manly deserves the recognition. For more about this man, see *Death Valley & the Amargosa* by Richard E. Lingenfelter.

If you follow this trail on to Zabriskie Point, you'll probably want to coordinate with another driver so that you don't have to retrace your route, for at this point you are 2.5 miles from the parking lot at Golden Canyon. If you do choose to retrace your steps, you have a hike of about 5 miles.

## Gower Gulch

The park provides yet another alternative for retracing your steps to Golden Canyon parking lot. When you reach the upper portions of Golden Canyon, you can pick up a trail (signed) that will take you down Gower Gulch and then return you to your vehicle, parked about half a mile away at the Golden Canyon parking lot. Another alternative is to make Gower Gulch a separate hike, striking out alone or joining the naturalist-led hike.

*Ranger Charlie Callagan leads a group into the canyon of Gower Gulch.*

Regardless of which way you elect to proceed, Gower Gulch is a spectacular canyon. Because there is no defined parking lot, the route gets less traffic, but it provides features that are equally interesting. Along the way there are several dry falls that may require some help from a hiking companion to navigate. Rain created the falls over the course of many years; today they are dry—except during flash floods, when they can be torrents.

As you climb through the winding and twisting canyon, you'll see evidence of high waters where they've created a bank. Flowers don't grow below these high-water lines (one occurred in 1998), but they do grow above the flood lines, even in a canyon where ground temperatures may approach 200 degrees Fahrenheit. Because of geological deposits in the area, you'll also see much evidence of mining activity in the gulch. Gower Gulch is rich in eroded material such as calcium, sodium, chlorine, sulfur, and boron. Under the sun's intense heat, "evaporites" formed as halite, gypsum, and borates. Remnant borax mines linger here, although for safety reasons you should avoid the shafts. Still, their existence recalls one of the park's most colorful eras.

The gulch also contains many of the features common to Golden Canyon, including ripple marks and abundant evidence of alluvial fans, deposition, flooding, and the creation of silt and conglomerate rocks. These features are there for any who take the time to simply poke around.

Don't hike in these or any canyons if a rare desert rainstorm is imminent. Not only can flash floods form suddenly but also rain can cause rocks to fall. As always, carry plenty of water—and you will definitely want to bring a camera for this wonderful hike.

**TYPE OF TRIP:** A loop drive, entirely on paved roads. Because the Artists Drive road is narrow and twisty and has sharp dips, large RVs, trailers, or buses are not recommended. The drive takes a minimum of thirty minutes, but plan to stay longer.

**DISTANCE:** The entrance to Artists Drive is about 11 miles from Furnace Creek. The one-way loop drive itself is 9 miles long.

**TYPE OF VEHICLE:** Passenger car.

**DIRECTIONS:** From Furnace Creek, travel south on California Highway 190 for 1.3 miles; turn right onto Badwater Road. Go approximately 9.7 miles to the signed left-hand turn onto Artists Drive.

**MAPS:** Park handout map; National Geographic/Trails Illustrated Topo Map 221.

## Description

Artists Drive is a "must-do" trip. Throughout the drive, you get the feeling that Mother Nature went above and beyond the call of beauty. Late afternoon, just before sunset, is the perfect time to be there. The setting sun illuminates the incredible colors, especially at Artists Palette.

This is also a place for learning about and viewing some of the park's fascinating geology, which is constantly changing. As you begin the drive, look to the right at the huge alluvial fan, coursing from the Black Mountains. The lack of vegetation on these mountains allows water to push rocks and soil down, forming the fan.

About 2 miles along, you'll come to a steep wash on the right. Water rushing from the mountains carves this wash ever deeper. Another 1.5 miles brings you to the sharp right turn to Artists Palette. Get out here and view the amazing array of colors. Walk

*Artists Palette provides a riot of colors.*

# Artists Drive

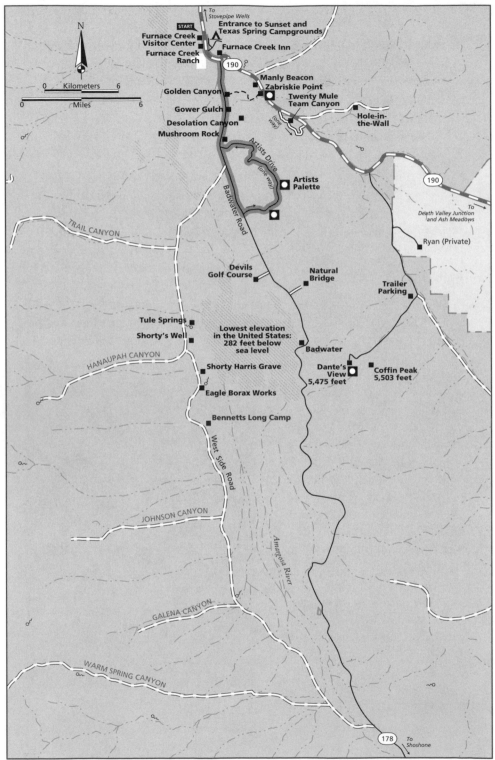

down among the rocks and wonder why these hues are grouped together here. Ancient peoples ground up the colored rocks and used them as a form of paint. Walk back to the interpretive sign and learn how mineral pigments such as iron, mica, and manganese have created the colors you see before you.

Toward the end of the drive, the road twists through hills made of deposits of gravel, sand, and boulders, called fanglomerates. Their golden hue at sunset offers yet another photographic opportunity.

There are many pullouts on this drive; feel free to get out of your vehicle and wander at will. This is one of the charming advantages to Death Valley—just being able to explore!

## Devils Golf Course

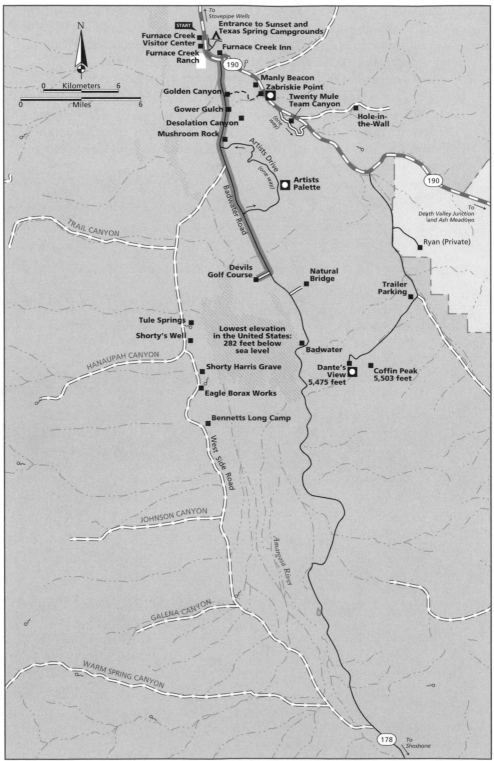

# 17 - Devils Golf Course

**TYPE OF TRIP:** Paved road drive until the final 1.3 miles of rough dirt road.

**DISTANCE:** 14.7 miles one-way from Furnace Creek.

**TYPE OF VEHICLE:** Passenger car.

**DIRECTIONS:** From Furnace Creek, travel south on California Highway 190 for 1.3 miles, and then turn right (south) onto Badwater Road. Go 12.2 miles and take the right-hand (signed) turn onto the dirt road to Devils Golf Course. Proceed for 1.3 miles to the parking area.

**MAPS:** Park handout map; National Geographic/Trails Illustrated Topo Map 221.

## Description

Many names in Death Valley National Park reflect upon devils and other ghoulish things. But this "golf course" could not be more aptly named, for it conjures up images of a mischievous devil having fun with all of us.

Two thousand years ago, a huge salt lake some 30 feet deep covered what is now known as the Devils Golf Course. Over the years the lake began to dry up, forming thick salty layers, which expanded and contracted from weathering. Then heat and an almost complete lack of humidity sucked all moisture from

*Devils Golf Course, dramatized by a rare rainfall in 2003. Eventually the water will evaporate and more crystals will form.*

the layers, transforming a salty muck into the incredible maze of salty shapes, angles, and sizes that now stretch before you. The salt is actually about 95 percent pure "table" salt. But don't "borrow" a crystal to take home—you'll find that it quickly breaks down, not to mention that it is illegal to remove items from the park. Rangers call all Death Valley rock "Leaverites," meaning "Leave her right there!" But you can certainly touch the crystals, and if you do you'll see how very sharp they are. This is not the place for moccasins or bare feet.

Today the valley is sinking (just as it has been for many millions of years), and the area is constantly changing as groundwater comes to the surface; as it evaporates it creates new crystals whiter than the older ones. Death Valley is a dynamic area, and the millennia have created one of the largest saltpans in North America. Come back in a thousand years and things here should look pretty much the same.

**TYPE OF TRIP:** A drive and an out-and-back, easy to moderate uphill hike. The road to Natural Bridge is paved until the signed turnoff to the canyon; then follow a short, rough dirt road to the parking lot. Plan on anywhere from a half hour to as much as three hours to explore.

**DISTANCE:** The drive is 16.6 miles one-way from Furnace Creek Visitor Center. The hike is a 1-mile round-trip to the bridge, a 2-mile round-trip to the end of the canyon.

**TYPE OF VEHICLE:** Passenger car.

**DIRECTIONS:** From Furnace Creek Visitor Center, go south on California Highway 190 for 1 mile to the right turn onto Badwater Road. Go 14.1 miles to the signed turnoff to Natural Bridge on the left (east). Travel 1.5 miles up a steep alluvial fan on a rather rough dirt road to the large parking area. The trail heads east from the information kiosk.

**MAPS:** Park handout; National Geographic/Trails Illustrated Topo Map 221.

## Description

Before embarking on the walk into the canyon, read the fascinating and important geologic history provided at the kiosk. Here the faulting, mud drips, dry

*Natural Bridge, created by erosion.*

# Natural Bridge

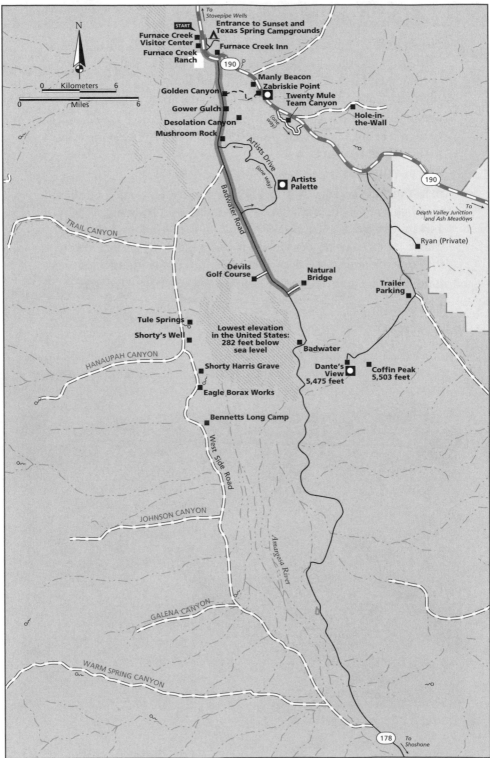

N

0 Kilometers 6

0 Miles 6

To Stovepipe Wells

START

Furnace Creek
Visitor Center

Entrance to Sunset and
Texas Spring Campgrounds

Furnace Creek
Ranch

Furnace Creek Inn

190

Golden Canyon

Manly Beacon
Zabriskie Point

Twenty Mule
Team Canyon

Hole-in-
the-Wall

Gower Gulch

Desolation Canyon

Mushroom Rock

Artists Drive
(one way)

Badwater Road

Artists
Palette

190

To
Death Valley Junction
and Ash Meadows

TRAIL CANYON

Ryan (Private)

Devils
Golf Course

Natural
Bridge

Trailer
Parking

Tule Springs

Shorty's Well

Lowest elevation
in the United States:
282 feet below
sea level

Badwater

Dante's
View
5,475 feet

Coffin Peak
5,503 feet

HANAUPAH CANYON

Shorty Harris Grave

Eagle Borax Works

Bennetts Long Camp

West Side Road

JOHNSON CANYON

Amargosa River

GALENA CANYON

WARM SPRING CANYON

178

To
Shoshone

falls, fracturing, tilting, and erosion you'll see are all well explained. Dangers of desert hiking are also spelled out quite succinctly: "Water and heat, rough terrain, spiny plants, poisonous critters, and flash floods."

You will come to the 50-foot natural bridge over the sandy, gravelly canyon in 0.5 mile. On the north side of the bridge are the old gullies where water coursed through years ago and eventually formed this phenomenon.

As you continue, the canyon widens, with mud walls on either side and mountains towering in the background. Mud drips are visible on the walls just past the bridge, as are some impressive fault caves.

At 0.8 mile, a pretty dry fall seems to block the way. It is climbable, but a bit slippery. However, 0.2 mile later, a huge dry fall totally blocks the way, and here you must turn around.

Exploring Natural Bridge is another Death Valley trip back in time. Forces are still at work in this lovely canyon. The views on the return trip are wonderful, especially on a clear day, as you look across Badwater to Telescope Peak and the rest of the Panamint Range.

# Badwater

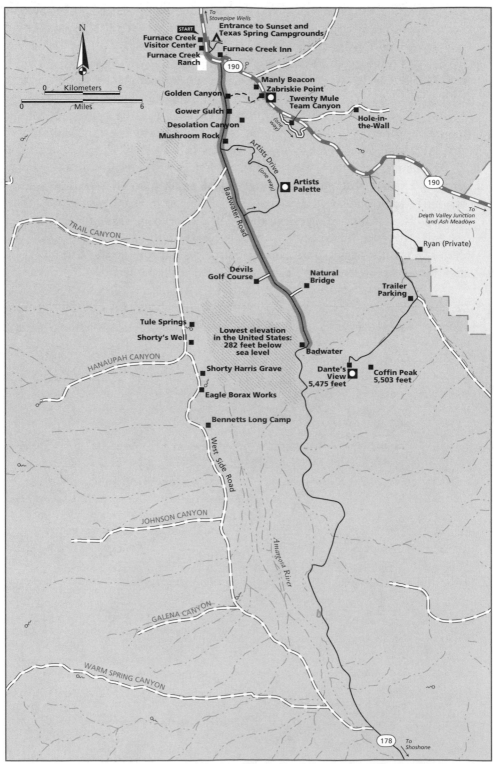

To Stovepipe Wells

N

START
Furnace Creek
Visitor Center

Entrance to Sunset and
Texas Spring Campgrounds

Furnace Creek Inn

Furnace Creek
Ranch

Kilometers    6

0        Miles        6

190

Manly Beacon
Zabriskie Point

Golden Canyon

Twenty Mule
Team Canyon

Gower Gulch

(one way)

Hole-in-
the-Wall

Desolation Canyon

Mushroom Rock

Artists Drive

(one way)

Artists
Palette

190

TRAIL CANYON

Badwater Road

To
Death Valley Junction
and Ash Meadows

Ryan (Private)

Devils
Golf Course

Natural
Bridge

Trailer
Parking

Tule Springs

Shorty's Well

Lowest elevation
in the United States:
282 feet below
sea level

Badwater

HANAUPAH CANYON

Shorty Harris Grave

Dante's
View
5,475 feet

Coffin Peak
5,503 feet

Eagle Borax Works

Bennetts Long Camp

West Side Road

JOHNSON CANYON

Amargosa River

GALENA CANYON

WARM SPRING CANYON

178

To
Shoshone

**TYPE OF TRIP:** Out-and-back drive on a paved road, with an optional hike of 1 to 2 miles. Do not make this hike in the summer heat.

**DISTANCE:** An 18-mile one-way drive from Furnace Creek.

**TYPE OF VEHICLE:** Passenger car.

**DIRECTIONS:** Drive 1.3 miles south from Furnace Creek on California Highway 190. Bear right on Badwater Road and travel south for 16.7 miles to the signed parking area for Badwater to the west.

**MAPS:** Park handout map; National Geographic/Trails Illustrated Topo Map 221.

## Description

Place your hand in the water at Badwater, taste your fingers, and you'll understand the name. The water here, however, is not really bad; it's just salty—about the same as the ocean, about 7 percent salt. Prospectors are responsible for the name; one man specifically watched as his mule refused to drink the "bad water." The water is not poisonous, as prospectors, probably ill from Epsom and Glauber's salts, may have believed.

Although the name has helped immortalize the area, Badwater is even better known as the lowest area in the Northern Hemisphere. The distinction did not come overnight. In 1861 Joel Brooks figured from early-day barometric readings that the area was 377 feet below sea level. Later those figures were revised to 100 feet below sea level. Ten years later, surveyors for the Southern Pacific Railroad took measurements in nearby Salton Sink that read –215. Back and forth the battle went for another ten years. In 1891 a botanical expedition reported areas in the Badwater to be –351 feet. Subsequent readings over the next ten to fifteen years pushed the depth down to –480 feet—great for an area trying to attract tourists, as it could claim yet another extreme. The figure changed again in 1907 when L. F. Bigger of the United States Geological Survey made calculations that set the depth at –276 feet. That measurement held until 1951, when the U.S. Geological Survey found two points that are –282 feet—the figure that has been accepted for over half a century.

But what about the Salton Sink? Throughout the early 1900s, surveyors variously provided depths ranging from –287 to –274 feet. True figures, however, will never be known; waters from the Colorado River filled the sink, transforming it into the Salton Sea, layered now with many sediments.

Today Badwater, with its –282-foot reading boasts the lowest elevation in the Western Hemisphere. The figure pales, however, when compared to the Dead Sea, which measures –1,312 feet. But as many naturalists point out in their talks, "The bedrock of Death Valley dips another 7,000 to 10,000 feet.

Strip the area of its loose fill of rock and silt, and Badwater would win hands down."

Today you cannot drive to the −282-foot point, and although naturalists conduct hikes along the boardwalk through the Badwater area, they do not take you to the low points. Nor are you encouraged to strike out for those areas on your own, since the area is so incredibly fragile. Please remain on the boardwalk.

**TYPE OF TRIP:** A loop drive, beginning and ending on paved roads; the West Side Road (the west side of this loop) is graded dirt. Plan on a full day for this trip. Have a full tank of gas, and take plenty of water, a camera, and emergency rations.

**DISTANCE:** The total loop is approximately 92 miles, including the 40-mile dirt portion of the trip.

**TYPE OF VEHICLE:** Although you may see passenger cars on the West Side Road, they are not encouraged. A high-clearance vehicle is preferred; if the road is wet, you'll need a four-wheel-drive vehicle. Check with a ranger or at the visitor center before departing on this, or any other, dirt-road trip.

**DIRECTIONS:** Directions for this drive begin from the southern end and proceed north. The road does not confine you to a single direction of travel. If you prefer, start from the northern end and follow the highlights in reverse.

From Furnace Creek, go south on California Highway 190 for 1.3 miles to the right (south) turn onto Badwater Road. Stay on Badwater Road for 44 miles. Three miles prior to Ashford Mill, there is a sign on the right for the graded dirt West Side Road. It is a hard right, and the road almost immediately goes due north. Stay on this road, stopping to explore the various offerings. At the end you'll be back on Badwater Road, 7 miles from Furnace Creek.

**MAPS:** Park handout map; National Geographic/Trails Illustrated Topo Map 221.

## Description

We made this trip three days after Death Valley had received one of its rare February rainstorms. To the west, water shimmered in the salt flats, making the initial part of the drive south on Badwater Road even more beautiful. Once past Badwater, the Black Mountains rise suddenly in front of you, a fascinating sight with the fault lines and alluvial fans. On the slopes of these mountains you can see "turtlebacks," a term applied to the "smoothed surface of a fault line between two blocks of crust." A good example is the 3-mile-long Mormon Point Turtleback, about 13 miles south of Badwater.

Two other places of interest lie just beyond the turnoff to the West Side Road: Shoreline Butte and the ruins of the Ashford Mill.

Because of the rains, our timing to the area was perfect. Proceeding along the West Side Road, in less than a mile we came to the Amargosa River. And it

# West Side Road

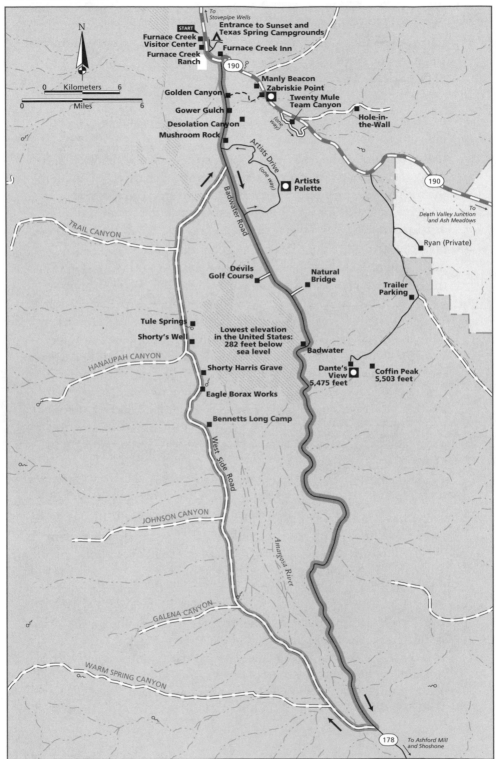

N

0 Kilometers 6

0 Miles 6

To
Stovepipe Wells

START

Furnace Creek
Visitor Center

Furnace Creek
Ranch

Entrance to Sunset and
Texas Spring Campgrounds

Furnace Creek Inn

190

Manly Beacon
Zabriskie Point
Twenty Mule
Team Canyon

Golden Canyon

Hole-in-
the-Wall

Gower Gulch

Desolation Canyon

Mushroom Rock

Artists Drive
(one way)

Artists
Palette

190

Badwater Road

To
Death Valley Junction
and Ash Meadows

TRAIL CANYON

Ryan (Private)

Devils
Golf Course

Natural
Bridge

Trailer
Parking

Tule Springs

Shorty's Well

Lowest elevation
in the United States:
282 feet below
sea level

Badwater

Dante's
View
5,475 feet

Coffin Peak
5,503 feet

HANAUPAH CANYON

Shorty Harris Grave

Eagle Borax Works

Bennetts Long Camp

West Side Road

JOHNSON CANYON

Amargosa River

GALENA CANYON

WARM SPRING CANYON

178

To Ashford Mill
and Shoshone

was *flowing!*—a rare occurrence indeed. On average, this "river" swells its banks but once every three to four years; February 2003 was one of those years. At such rare times, the Amargosa flows south from Nevada. It turns and enters Death Valley at the southern extreme of the valley, where it then turns north—eventually to flow into the salt flats, where the desert dryness removes the moisture, eventually evaporating a flow that can in places be violent.

On the day of our visit, the river was about 15 feet wide and covered the road. Some folks were hesitant to drive across, but the water was only wide, not deep, and no one had trouble. One prudent young man, however, asked his lady friend to test the waters, which she found to be calf deep. Because Death Valley is broad here, it would have indeed been surprising to find high water. However, in other parts of the park where canyons are narrow, floodwater can rise dozens of feet in a matter of hours.

After a few miles you'll pass Warm Spring Canyon on the left, and then Galena Canyon at Mile 10.5. At Miles 13 to 15, look to your right to see the huge alluvial fan, backdropped by a palette of variegated colors in the Black Mountains to the east. Soon you'll find the road you're traveling is nearly in the center of the valley. Here you get a completely different perspective of the Panamints and the Amargosa Range. You'll soon come to perceive just how huge this valley really is.

About 15 miles from the road's beginning, the road to Johnson Canyon intersects from the west. This much more rugged road, about 10 miles long, takes you to Hungry Bill's Ranch.

About 20 miles in, you come to Bennetts Long Camp to the east. Here in 1849 the stranded forty-niners waited and prayed for the return of William Manly and John Rogers. Trying to find a route through Death Valley, the group had exhausted their supply of food.

Not everyone in the group, at what is now Bennetts Long Camp, waited. Several persons struck out on their own. Richard Culverwell, who had joined the impatient ones, realized he was too weak to travel and turned back to the Bennette-Arcane camp. He died several miles short of the camp and was later found on his back, arms extended, with a canteen made from a powder keg lying by his side.

Rogers and Manly, who had succeeded in reaching San Fernando, were the men who found Culverwell. Some might have called it quits and, in fact, several in the Bennette-Arcane party later said they thought the men would be crazy to return. But Rogers and Manly obtained the necessary supplies and returned to Death Valley, and their feat now ranks as one of American history's more heroic exploits.

Today Death Valley honors these heroes, paying homage by attaching their names to some of the park's most beautiful and significant features. Not far

*Grave of "Shorty" Harris on West Side Road.*

from Furnace Creek, Manly Beacon juts up from the area around Zabriskie Point. The ancient seabed that once covered Death Valley is named Lake Manly. And not far from the Charcoal Kilns is Rogers Peak.

At Mile 23.6 you'll see the old site of Eagle Borax Works. Although it carries the distinction of being the first of the valley's borax mines, it closed within two years. Take time to walk around. More than likely you'll find the tracks of a kit fox or coyote. The abundant vegetation in the area, which feeds smaller mammals, attracts such predators to the area. Look long enough and you may find dens, with droppings and seedpods deposited all around.

The grave of famed miner Shorty Harris is on the right at Mile 24.6 (unsigned). He asked that he be buried with his best friend, and the two of them are still together in a beautiful spot in their favorite desert area. The graves are about 20 yards off the road, marked by a rock cairn structure with the inscription:

BURY ME BESIDE JIM DAYTON IN THE VALLEY WE LOVED. ABOVE ME WRITE: "HERE LIES SHORTY HARRIS, A SINGLE BLANKET JACKASS PROSPEC-TOR BELOVED GOLD HUNTER. 1865 TO 1934. HERE JAS. DAYTON PIONEER PERISHED 1898."

At Mile 26 you'll see a sign for Shorty's Well. The road to Shorty's Well is on the right, a short distance past Hanaupah Canyon Road, on the left. It may take a bit of searching to find the well—it is in the bushes just where the dirt side road ends. All the vegetation along the east side of the road for the past several miles indicates that it is quite wet along here.

Tule Springs is on the right at Mile 27.5; take the dirt road just past the sign. Arrowweed thrives here in this wet, salty place and makes another "Devil's Cornfield." After Tule Springs the greenery becomes sparse.

The sign for Trail Canyon is at Mile 32.1, and the road is just ahead on the left (west). Hikers can reach Aguereberry Point from this canyon.

Trail Canyon is the last turnoff from West Side Road, which suddenly winds through the Devils Golf Course and puts you back on the paved Badwater Road near Artists Drive at Mile 37.6. Turn left (north) onto Badwater Road to return to Furnace Creek.

# Hikes and Drives East, Southwest, and North of Stovepipe Wells

## 21 - Death Valley Dunes and Devil's Cornfield

**TYPE OF TRIP:** An out-and-back drive on a paved road, with optional hikes in the dunes and Devil's Cornfield.

**DISTANCE:** From Stovepipe Wells, the out-and-back drive on the paved road is 9.4 miles. Hiking distances are up to you.

**TYPE OF VEHICLE:** Passenger car.

**DIRECTIONS:** From the village of Stovepipe Wells, go east on California Highway 190. The sand dunes lie 2 miles away on the west side of the road. Devil's Cornfield is 2.7 miles past the sand dunes.

**MAPS:** Park handout map; National Geographic/Trails Illustrated Topo Map 221.

## Description

The Death Valley Sand Dunes are the most visible and easily accessible dunes in the valley. The best access is along CA 190 east of Stovepipe Wells. This trip is a great family outing—the children can run barefoot to their hearts' content, and looking for tracks in the sand, especially in early morning, involves everyone. When temperatures are hot, carry your shoes with you, as well as plenty of water.

Formed about 10,000 years ago, in the present era (the Cenozoic), these dunes receive a lot of wind and therefore sand deposits, but they actually change very little from year to year, even though the sand shifts so much. Although not very high, the dunes spread over approximately 14 miles. Three types of dunes are in this field: crescent, linear, and star-shaped. Walk to the top of one, especially at dusk, and you'll see how discernible the shapes are.

Dunes need sand and wind to become what they are. The shapes found here are such because the wind blows so strongly from one direction (the southwest). The tiny grains of sand that make up this ocean of dunes could tell of an amazing history and journey to their present resting place. Geologists say that most of the grains came from quartz fragments, perhaps a billion years old, that once were larger rocks buried miles beneath the earth's surface until they were uplifted as part of an ancient mountain. And here these grains exist today, providing shelter for many animals and beauty for us.

# *Death Valley Dunes and Devil's Cornfield*

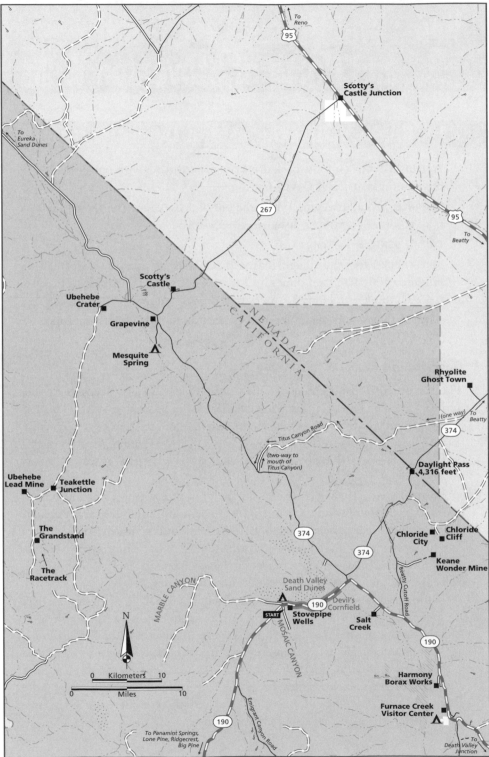

To Reno

95

Scotty's
Castle Junction

267

95

To
Beatty

To
Eureka
Sand Dunes

Scotty's
Castle

Ubehebe
Crater

Grapevine

NEVADA
CALIFORNIA

Mesquite
Spring

Rhyolite
Ghost Town

(one way)    To
Beatty

374

Titus Canyon Road

(two-way to
mouth of
Titus Canyon)

Daylight Pass
4,316 feet

Ubehebe
Lead Mine

Teakettle
Junction

The
Grandstand

374

Chloride
City

Chloride
Cliff

374

Keane
Wonder Mine

The
Racetrack

MARBLE CANYON

Death Valley
Sand Dunes

190

Devil's
Cornfield

Beatty Cutoff Road

N

START

MOSAIC CANYON

Stovepipe
Wells

Salt
Creek

190

0    Kilometers    10

0         Miles         10

Harmony
Borax Works

Emigrant Canyon Road

190

To Panamint Springs,
Lone Pine, Ridgecrest,
Big Pine

Furnace Creek
Visitor Center

To
Death Valley
Junction

Mornings are a good time to visit here; the dune-dwellers are active during the cool nights and leave their telltale tracks for morning explorers to discover. Observing the animals themselves is rare, but in the evenings you might spot a kangaroo rat scurrying under the bushes or a coyote looking for prey. Lizards and birds also leave marks of their passing; if you are very lucky, you might see the distinctive trail of the sidewinder rattlesnake. Watch for wavy parallel lines scooting across the sand. Tracks are best found near the dense clumps of mesquite trees, which produce the seeds that kangaroo rats and insects love. If you're observant and spend some time here, you'll discover how this web of life works.

*Playa at Death Valley Dunes, near Stove-pipe Wells.*

Early morning and late afternoon are the best photo times. Each offers a different play of light on these beautiful dunes. Another hint: Why not view the dunes by moonlight?

Devil's Cornfield is aptly named. Huge shocks, which are really the plant arrowweed, grow here in this overly salty area—and they really do look like corn-shocks till you get close. Soil erosion causes the plants to grow in such weird clumps. The plant's roots can reach the saline water, which is fairly close to the surface. Indians depended on the arrowweed plant, as the strong, straight stems made good arrow shafts. This is a fun area to wander and view another Death Valley rarity.

*Marble Canyon*

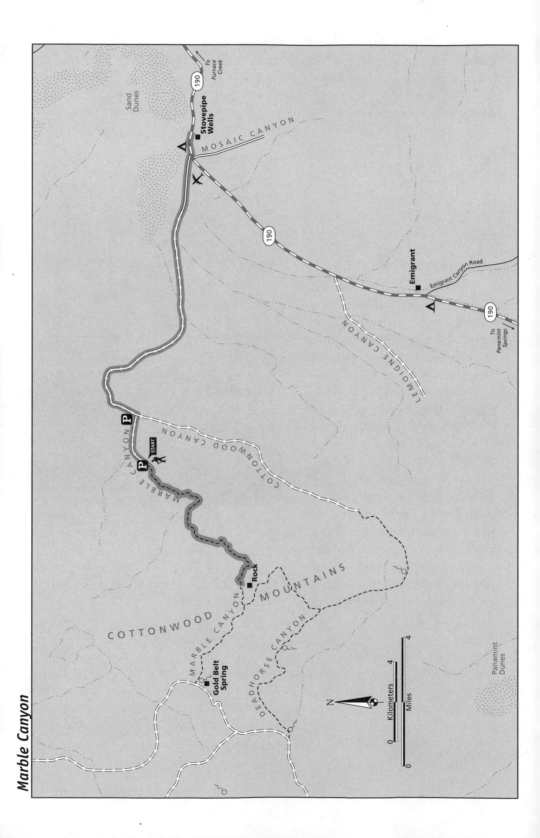

**TYPE OF TRIP:** An out-and-back drive and hike consisting entirely of backcountry roads. Plan on at least half a day or more, and be sure to have plenty of gas, water, food, and sunscreen. And bring your camera.

**DISTANCE:** From Stovepipe Wells on California Highway 190, the round-trip drive is 26.6 miles. How far into the canyons you hike is up to you. We made our turnaround at the sign for Gold Belt Spring, making our total hike 4 to 5 miles.

**TYPE OF VEHICLE:** A high-clearance two-wheel drive will get you to the junction of Marble and Cottonwood Canyons; you'll probably need four-wheel drive to manage the remaining 2.6 miles.

**DIRECTIONS:** From the village of Stovepipe Wells on CA 190, go left at the entrance to the Stovepipe Wells Campground. This is Cottonwood Creek Road. Follow it to the small aircraft landing strip, and then bear right. At 8.4 miles you'll come to an information sign. Here the road drops and goes south (left) into Cottonwood Canyon. The park advises high-clearance, four-wheel drive from this point on; the next 2.6 miles to the parking place has soft sand and is quite rocky. Park at the canyon narrows (at the CLOSED TO VEHICLES sign) to begin your hike.

**MAPS:** Park handout map; National Geographic/Trails Illustrated Topo Map 221; USGS Cottonwood Creek quad.

## Description

When asked about canyons in Death Valley, park naturalists say that one of their favorites is Marble Canyon in the Cottonwood Mountains outside Stovepipe Wells because of its isolation and its water-polished marble that shines with such brightness it almost seems a mirror. Naturalists also like this place because it is cool in the canyon when other areas may be hot. In spring the washes leading into and out of the canyon can be carpeted with flowers.

Marble Canyon is also fairly accessible, located as it is on a gravel road that originates near the campground at Stovepipe Wells. The road leads into the Cottonwood Mountains of the Panamint Range and begins with about 6 miles of sand that is relatively driver-friendly. After that, the drive becomes more challenging; you must navigate your vehicle through washes flanked on either side with high sand-and-gravel walls. Some of the wash sides on the left jut upward more than 7 feet high, and in places it seems as though rocks protruding from the bank might tumble at any moment. On the other side, conditions are a bit more accommodating; there are lots of holly and creosote bushes with their trademark yellow flowers that can seem so friendly. But don't become complacent; those loose rocks along your route indicate that on more than one occasion, the road has been inundated with water—at times, lots of it. In fact, all those loose rocks suggest that the force of water here has been enormous.

Eight and a half miles from the start, you'll arrive at an information sign. Here the road drops into Cottonwood Wash and then turns left up the canyon. For nearly 1 mile you'll travel through high walls and around large boulders. Soon you'll break into the open, but your drive through rock-strewn washes goes on.

At 10.7 miles from Stovepipe Wells, the road to Marble Canyon goes right and the Cottonwood road goes left. At the V a cobbled-together sign marks the routes. Because we drive in an extraordinarily prudent manner, it took us about one to one and a half hours to reach this point, leaving us with another 2.6 miles to reach the trailhead.

You'll see that the mountains to the west are dramatically upthrust. As evidenced by the very conspicuous lines, the layers here have been almost vertically oriented. Adding to the drama are the mountains just ahead, which tantalize with their coats of many colors. We crept along in our high four-wheel-drive truck, requiring an additional twenty-five minutes to cover these last few miles. Despite the crowded campgrounds back at Furnace Creek and Stovepipe Wells, on this day the only other car out here was a low-slung Subaru that seemed to have survived the trip quite well.

Road's end is the trail's beginning, and the area seems to be excellent desert bighorn country. The rocks thrust upward and the area seems to provide not only vegetation but also good escape terrain. From this point on you're on a trail and in an officially designated wilderness area. Soon you enter Marble Canyon proper, which contains huge towering walls of shiny rock on either side. As your hike progresses, gray walls move in to engulf you. Veins of gold color stream vertically, adding to the beauty. If you lay your hand on the rock, you'll find that it's cool, perhaps even cold.

About a half mile after departing the trailhead, you come to some marred petroglyphs on the right and located at about eye level. From here the canyon presses in and the walls almost seem to touch. All the while, you are gradually ascending; if you look up, you can see caves all about.

After about 1.6 miles, the canyon suddenly yawns and you enter a wide-open area. This lasts only 0.3 mile before the canyon narrows once again. Look here for petroglyphs on both your right and left. Some are of sheep, but unfortunately, they, too, have been vandalized; it is difficult to make out the details.

Right after the petroglyphs the canyon opens and becomes a wide gravel wash. A major canyon enters here from the right, and for most this junction represents the turnaround point. The point is further demarcated by the

*Marble Canyon is a favorite park destination. The narrow, high walls provide part of the attraction.*

wooden etching of some unknown scribe, who wrote GOLD BELT SPRING 4 MILE into the desert varnish. The person included an arrow pointing to Marble Canyon on the right, which, if followed, would take you to Gold Belt Spring. Although we turned around at this point, you may want to continue. If you do, you have several alternatives. Go left (or south) and you'll pick up Dead Horse Canyon, also to the south, about 2 miles farther along. Ultimately the trail will take you into Cottonwood Canyon, but now you're beginning to enter the realm of a backpack trip. The other option is to go right toward Gold Belt Spring, which is, as the etching states, about 4 miles farther.

Most will want to turn around at the etching on the rock, which still makes for a respectable day's outing, particularly when you consider all the driving. Because of directional orientation, the sun seems to work to your advantage— it is at your back both going in and coming out.

**TYPE OF TRIP:** Out-and-back hike.

**DISTANCE:** 2.4 miles round-trip.

**DIRECTIONS:** The signed rough dirt road to Mosaic Canyon is 0.1 mile south of Stovepipe Wells, on the left. The road is about 2 miles long, with a parking lot provided. The trail heads south into the canyon.

**MAPS:** Park handout map; National Geographic/Trails Illustrated Topo Map 221.

## Description

Mosaic Canyon was formed long ago from a fault in Tucki Mountain and covers 4 square miles in this range.

The hike starts with an examination of the abundant conglomerate rocks, which are about 25 yards up the canyon. They suggest flooding on different scales; some were large floods, others were small. There's also evidence of mudflows, which are rather recent, in the past five to ten years.

Once again, Charlie Callagan is our guide, and he creates a relaxed atmosphere by inviting a young child to help him out. The young boy, about five years old, has lots of questions—too many—but Charlie either incorporates the

*Mosaic Canyon provides views of marble, colorful rocks, geological formations, and great beauty.*

# Mosaic Canyon

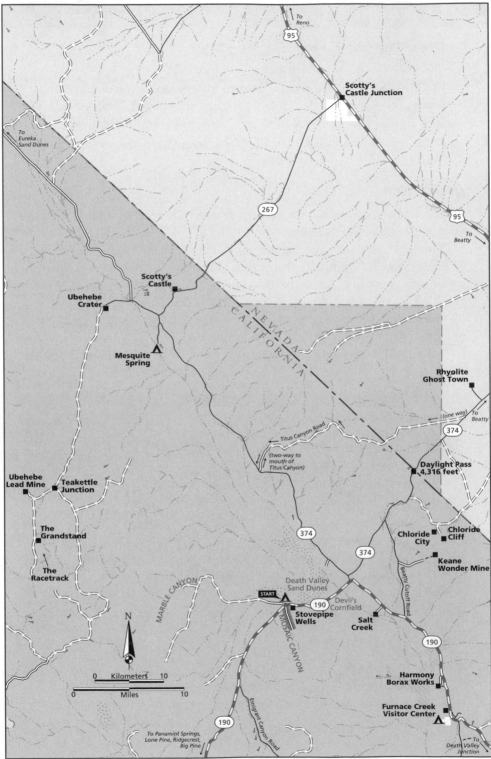

To Reno

95

Scotty's
Castle Junction

267

95

To
Beatty

To
Eureka
Sand Dunes

Scotty's
Castle

Ubehebe
Crater

NEVADA
CALIFORNIA

Mesquite
Spring

Rhyolite
Ghost Town

(one way) To
Beatty

374

Titus Canyon Road

(two-way to
mouth of
Titus Canyon)

Daylight Pass
4,316 feet

Ubehebe
Lead Mine

Teakettle
Junction

The
Grandstand

374

Chloride
City

Chloride
Cliff

Keane
Wonder Mine

The
Racetrack

374

MARBLE CANYON

Death Valley
Sand Dunes

START

190

Devil's
Cornfield

Beatty Cutoff Road

N

MOSAIC CANYON

Stovepipe
Wells

Salt
Creek

190

0    Kilometers    10

0         Miles         10

Harmony
Borax Works

Furnace Creek
Visitor Center

190

To Panamint Springs,
Lone Pine, Ridgecrest,
Big Pine

Emigrant Canyon Road

190

To
Death Valley
Junction

questions into the group discussion or deflects them in a way that brings laughs, but not at the child's expense.

The next stop, about 25 yards along, dramatizes the forces within the earth's surface. Here are large blocks of rock that have been separated and then sheered from one another until there's a visible separation. The horizon brown depositions in one block now are elevated above the brown depositions in the other block by about 12 to 15 feet. The power of the forces underlying these blocks is dramatic.

Moving along we stop at a wall of pure marble. The marble is a rather subdued off-white, but when Charlie pours water over the rock, it brightens with rosy hues. "Mosaic always seems to change," says Charlie. "As many times as I've been here, I've never seen it look the same." We continue our stroll up the narrow canyon, stopping at a metal railing that must have once been needed for hiking up the canyon safely. "When I first came here," Charlie relates, "these steps were distinct. But as you can see, they've been washed away. More has happened, too. Waters eroded the rock, widening the canyon and making passage through this section quite easy. Obviously, it wasn't always this way."

At the next stop, perhaps another 25 yards up the canyon, we see where mud has spackled the wall about 20 feet above the floor of the narrow canyon. The mud hasn't been there too long, perhaps five years, but its presence speaks of great volumes of water pouring through the canyon—"enough," says Charlie, "to float a raft." The mud won't last forever, but it tells a story of high water and the infrequency of such gully washes.

At another stop we see how the water was altered by a change in the structure of the canyon. Where we're standing, the canyon is broad, perhaps a hundred yards or more in width. But then the canyon suddenly constricts. Any water pouring through here would have been slowed, for the narrow canyon would have served as a partial dam, causing the flood waters to rise. With the rise, the waters would have left mud at their highest level. Charlie believes that these waters were not part of the wash of several years ago; rather they're from an earlier time, perhaps twenty-five to fifty years ago.

As we gain a slight bit of elevation, we see a few plants, but all are the same species, a rock nettle. Locally, natives refer to the plant as the "Velcro plant," for if you brush against its leaves, they'll stick like Velcro.

In a pinch, sheep will eat rock nettle, although they prefer the other plants that are found in the area, such as honey sweet and desert trumpet. The presence of vegetation and the steep landscape make this perfect sheep habitat—as long as there's water, which Charlie says there is.

Just after the narrows, we enter a broad area where several washes converge. Large rocks hang overhead. Charlie was here during the Landers Earthquake. The next day he wandered up Mosaic Canyon and found that many boulders had fallen from overhead and now littered the canyon floor. Because we're standing in the shade and are still feeling the effects of the cold (about 30 degrees Fahrenheit), we move into the sun. Nearby is a trail the miners used. We follow it back to our vehicle.

On a previous trip, we continued up Mosaic Canyon, coming to a dry fall about a mile up the canyon. The fall wasn't a high one, but adjacent to the left (east), a path through several boulders provided access to the canyon and a continuation of the hike until, about 0.75 mile farther, we were stopped by a 75-foot dry fall.

Mosaic is a delight!

As with most places in the park, don't hike here if rain threatens. Carry lots of water and sunscreen, wear a hat—and don't forget your camera.

**TYPE OF TRIP:** A loop or out-and-back drive to Skidoo townsite, Eureka Mine, Aguereberry Point, and the Charcoal Kilns with much back-country driving, beginning and ending on paved roads. You should plan on a full day for this trip, so take food, water, sun protection, a camera, and plenty of gas.

**DISTANCE:** If you elect to make this a loop drive from Stovepipe Wells, the distance is approximately 98 miles, including all stops mentioned. If you decide to backtrack your route to Stovepipe Wells, the distance is about 96 miles.

**TYPE OF VEHICLE:** This trip entails driving over some very rough, wash-board-type roads. High-clearance and/or four-wheel-drive vehicles are certainly useful, but not a necessity. *No trailers longer than 25 feet are permitted once you leave California Highway 190.*

**DIRECTIONS:** The starting point for this trip is from Stovepipe Wells on CA 190, located 26 miles northwest of Furnace Creek. The specific directions to the various places planned for the trip will be provided in the following write-up.

**MAPS:** Park handout map; National Geographic/Trails Illustrated Topo Map 221.

## Description

Depart south from Stovepipe Wells Village on CA 190 toward Emigrant. You'll come to Emigrant Campground (tenting only) on the right after 10 miles. Just past the campground, take the paved Emigrant Canyon Road on the left (south-east) and travel 10 miles to a dirt road on the left (east), leading to Skidoo townsite (no trailers, no camping). Now the fun begins. This narrow, twisty dirt road can be extremely rough if not recently graded. Along the way you'll see abandoned mines, old structures, and lots of rusted mining artifacts. You can pull off and explore, but do not enter mineshafts or structures or remove anything.

After nearly 8 miles of jouncing up the road, you reach Skidoo and see— virtually nothing. The town is gone, but in its heyday around 1907, it housed 700 persons who worked the hundreds of gold mines in the area. Skidoo boasted a bank, a school, and a telephone. How, we wondered, did these rugged people haul water and necessities to this stark place? Perhaps the beautiful views of the Panamint Range helped compensate for the harshness.

After exploring at will, return down the same road and turn left on Emigrant Road. Go for about 2 miles to another dirt-road turnoff on the left (east) leading to Aguereberry Point. Even though this can be another rough ride, we

# Emigrant Road

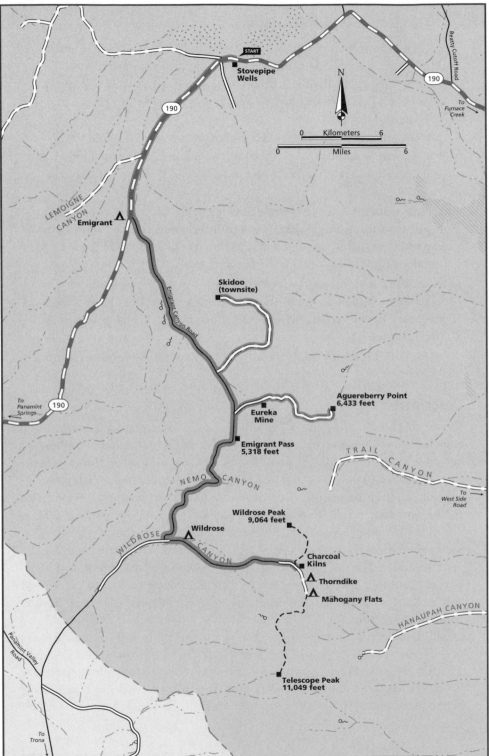

START
Stovepipe Wells

190

N

0    Kilometers    6
0    Miles    6

190
To Furnace Creek

Beatty Cutoff Road

LEMOIGNE CANYON

Emigrant

Emigrant Canyon Road

Skidoo (townsite)

Aguereberry Point
6,433 feet

To Panamint Springs
190

Eureka Mine

Emigrant Pass
5,318 feet

TRAIL CANYON

To West Side Road

NEMO CANYON

Wildrose Peak
9,064 feet

Wildrose

WILDROSE CANYON

Charcoal Kilns

Thorndike

Mahogany Flats

HANAUPAH CANYON

Panamint Valley Road

Telescope Peak
11,049 feet

To Trona

consider this trip (2 miles to Eureka Mine and 4 more miles to Aguereberry Point) to be a "don't miss" drive through designated wilderness.

After 2 miles you'll reach Aguereberry Camp and the Eureka Mine on the right. Pull into the camp and explore-walk east to the mine and the old mill. An interpretive sign at the mine explains that an endangered winged mammal winters here (the Townsend big-eared bat) and that the mine is closed at times to protect the species. When the mine is open, you are also advised to use caution while exploring. Take two flashlights, cautions the sign, ONE FOR USE, ONE FOR BACKUP.

Leaving Aguereberry Camp, continue for 4 miles on the rough dirt road to Aguereberry Point (elevation 6,433 feet). The road ascends shortly and then enters a beautiful canyon that winds steeply to the summit. Explorers won't want to miss the spectacular, nearly 360-degree views; enduring the rough ride is worth every mile! It is said that Pete Aguereberry built the first route to the point so that he could share the vistas with others.

To continue on to the Charcoal Kilns, return to Emigrant Canyon Road and turn left, driving over Emigrant Pass (elevation 5,318 feet). After 10 miles follow the sign on the left (east) to Wildrose Campground (free, water and pit toilets). Continue 6 more miles (the last 3 or 4 miles are *very* rough) to the Charcoal Kilns.

Appearing suddenly like ten huge beehives, each kiln is 25 feet high, about 30 feet in diameter, and approximately 25 inches thick at the base, tapering to perhaps 12 inches at the top. According to park literature, these structures may be the best-preserved charcoal kilns in the West, perhaps in part because they are so isolated and were in operation for only three years. In 1970 the kilns became part of the Park Service's Historic Structures Preservation Program. In 1971 a team of Arizona Navajo Indians labored in horrific weather to restore and stabilize the kilns, preserving what you see today.

Making charcoal is an ancient, exact, and time-consuming project. You'll note that the area is blanketed with piñon pine, the perfect wood to turn into charcoal. The pine was cut and hauled to the kilns, and about four cords of wood were burned at a time in each kiln. Two more weeks were then needed for the wood to cool and become charcoal. "Why this immense labor project?" you might ask. Thirty miles to the west of Wildrose Canyon was the Modoc Mine, producing gold and ore, and the slow-burning charcoal was needed to run the smelters at the mine.

After all the labor of building the kilns and the road out of the canyon and cutting the trees—after all this, the smelters were abandoned by 1885. It is believed that the kilns operated only from perhaps 1877 to 1880. But these wonderful reminders of the past make one realize that the Death Valley miners were a hardy, ingenious lot.

## Aguereberry Point—A Mighty Fine View

On January 20 we arose about 4:00 A.M. to watch the sunrise from Aguereberry Point. The road was washboardy, and near the top it was so narrow that it was suitable for single-line traffic only.

The view from the top of Aguereberry Point is extraordinary—in all directions. You can see the Salt Flats, Badwater, and all the area's major mountain ranges—although you can't see Telescope Peak from here. As we stood in the predawn darkness, the rocks were monochromatic, but as the sun appeared, the colors changed dramatically. It was a mighty fine view indeed.

Prospector Pete Aguereberry built the first route to the point, which he called "Fine View," and encouraged others to join him on trips from his mine to the promontory overlooking Death Valley. Aguereberry was one of the most recognized Death Valley prospectors, not because of his wealth but because of his tenacity. In fact, he might have worked his claim longer than any other prospector of the time—about forty years, until his death in 1945.

Aguereberry was born in France in 1874. At the age of fifteen he read about the gold discovery in California and begged his father to let him come to the United States. For several years he strove to learn English as he worked a variety of jobs, including herding sheep and driving a stagecoach and a milk truck. In 1902 he moved to Goldfield; in 1905 he attempted to cross Death Valley—and almost died. Oscar Denton found him and nursed him back to health. One month later Aguereberry met Shorty Harris, and together the two struck out for the "fleshpots" of Ballarat. Their route took them through the Panamints and then up toward Wildrose Spring. At the base of the little hills, Aguereberry picked up a rock and turned to Harris, who is reported to have said, "Hell! It's lousy with gold." Aguereberry suggested that they stake out a claim, but Harris replied, "We'll come back and do it. If we don't get to Ballarat tomorrow night, all the likker will be gone."

The following evening Aguereberry listened in horror as a loose-tongued Harris boasted of a find in the Panamints. Several days later the pair returned to their site and discovered that others had intruded on their claim. Somehow the pair reasserted their claim, and although Harris sold his claim several years later, Aguereberry retained his and began work that he followed for about forty years. Over the years Aguereberry installed air pumps, a baby-gauge railroad, and compressed air drills. He also built a home that still stands at the west end of the complex. Today much of what he constructed persists—as does the general route (now vastly improved) to his "Fine View."

*These charcoal kilns, used between 1877 and 1880, are the West's best preserved. Slow-burning charcoal produced here fired smelters.*

The kilns are extremely photogenic, but the hills to their east keep them in the shadows until midafternoon. Shadows block them again in the late afternoon.

***Hiking note:*** The Wildrose Peak trailhead (a 4.2-mile one-way trek) is beside the first kiln as you drive into the area. This trail is one of two maintained trails in the park, the other being Telescope Peak, which is 1.6 miles farther past the kilns at Mahogany Flat Campground.

As you retrace the road out of Wildrose Canyon, you have two choices. You can simply return by the same routes (Emigrant Canyon Road to CA 190 to Stovepipe Wells), or you can make a loop back to Stovepipe Wells (all on paved roads). To make the loop, take a left turn just past the Wildrose Campground at the sign for Trona; you will travel through Wildrose Canyon (no vehicles over 25 feet allowed). After 9 miles take the first paved road on your right; this is Panamint Valley Road. Continue for about 12 miles until you come to a T-intersection (CA 190). Go right (northeast) for 26 miles to Stovepipe Wells. The loop drive is a few miles longer but is scenic and wonderful for afternoon photography. In addition, traveling the loop affords a better understanding of the depth and scope of the park. You can get a different perspective of the Panamint Mountains to the east as you travel through Panamint Valley and enjoy a view of the "backside" of Telescope Peak.

# Telescope Peak

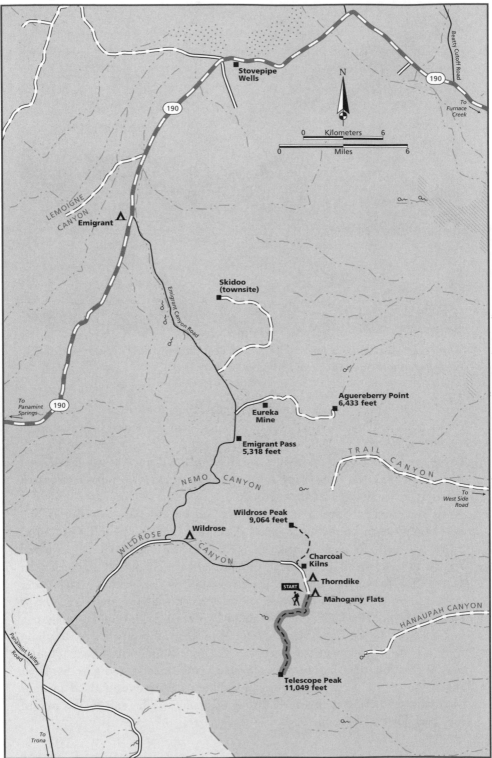

**TYPE OF TRIP:** Strenuous, all-day hike with an elevation gain of 2,916 feet.

**DISTANCE:** 14-mile round-trip hike.

**DIRECTIONS:** From Stovepipe Wells Campground, located on California Highway 190 (in west central Death Valley), travel southwest on CA 190 for 9.2 miles to Emigrant Canyon Road on your left. This will take you through Wildrose Canyon. Follow this road for a total of 30.5 miles until you reach Mahogany Flats Campground, where the road ends. Along the way you will have crossed Emigrant Pass, traveled through Nemo Canyon, and passed Wildrose Campground and Ranger Station. The pavement ends 9 miles past Wildrose Campground, at the Charcoal Kilns. A four-wheel-drive vehicle is best for the last few remaining miles, but this rough dirt road is accessible (when dry) by car or small van. Upon arrival at Mahogany Flats Campground parking lot, look uphill to the right to locate the Telescope Peak trailhead. *NOTE:* During winter the road above Charcoal Kilns is often closed by snow; hikers will have to trek an additional 3 miles uphill to the trailhead.

**MAPS:** National Geographic/Trails Illustrated Topo Map 221; USGS Telescope Peak 7.5-minute quad; USGS Emigrant Canyon 7.5-minute quad, 861.

## Description

Sometimes just reaching wilderness is a challenge. But therein lies the beauty. The Telescope Peak hike is just such a challenge, both in the getting there and in the hike through the Panamint Mountains to the peak of Death Valley's mountain monarch. On days when temperatures are soaring down on the valley floor, this hike can be particularly refreshing. With an elevation of 11,049 feet, Telescope Peak is one of the few recommended summer hikes. Plan on a full day, or about nine hours, for the trip.

The trail begins with an immediate ascent at a 9 percent grade. As you climb the narrow dirt path cut into the side of the hills, spectacular vistas open. Stands of mountain mahogany and piñon pine trees grow here, as well as bushes of sage and rabbitbrush.

Just prior to where the trail levels briefly to cross Arcane Meadows at Mile 3, take a short break to enjoy the view. From here you can see into the northern and southern reaches of Death Valley while relishing the sweeping majesty of the Amargosa Range. Directly across the valley to the east lies Badwater, which at 282 feet below sea level, is the lowest point in the United States. The contrast is amazing as you perhaps sit by a snow patch, looking at the shimmering desert floor.

The trail ascends once again and does so continuously for 4 more miles and 1,400 more feet to the summit; the final mile is quite steep. As you approach the peak, watch for bristlecone pine trees. Core samplings of species from other areas indicate that some of these timberline ancients can date back to 5,000 B.C. The age of the bristlecones on Telescope Peak has not been determined.

Storms can blow in suddenly over the Panamints; be sure to carry rain gear, warm clothes, and sufficient water. Backcounty camping, with free permit, is allowed 2 miles past the trailhead. However, be aware that most of this trail follows an exposed ridgeline.

Warnings are also issued that this hike can be extremely hazardous during the winter months (November until April) due to snow and ice. Only experienced climbers should be on the trail during this time, and they should be equipped with ice axes, crampons, and ropes. Those hiking during this period are required to check in with the ranger at Wildrose Ranger Station.

If you find these winter conditions existing even later into the spring season, and the road from the Charcoal Kilns to Mahogany Flats Campground is closed, a shorter alternative hike exists: Wildrose Peak. This 4.2-mile one-way trail is accessed at the west end of the Charcoal Kilns and takes four to six hours to complete the trip. The trail climbs approximately 2,264 feet through piñon pines and juniper and offers wonderful views in all directions.

Water is not available at the campground, the kilns, or along the trails. Dogs are not allowed on either trail.

**TYPE OF TRIP:** An out-and-back drive, mostly on paved highway, with 3 miles of good dirt road into the ghost town.

**DISTANCE:** 53.5 miles one-way from Stovepipe Wells, 30 miles one-way from Panamint Springs Resort.

**TYPE OF VEHICLE:** Passenger car.

**DIRECTIONS:** From Stovepipe Wells go south on California Highway 190 for 26 miles to the junction with Panamint Valley Road on the left (south). Follow Panamint Valley Road for 14.3 miles to stop sign. Turn right (south) on California Highway 178 for 9.7 miles to the sign for Ballarat. Turn left here and go 3.5 miles to the town.

From Panamint Springs go south on CA 190 for 2.5 miles and follow the directions above, beginning on Panamint Valley Road.

**MAPS:** Park handout map; Trails Illustrated/National Geographic Topo Map 221.

## Description

Although Ballarat is not in the park, we've included it here because it borders the park's southwest side and has played such an important part in the park's mining history. On the drive into the town, notice the salt flats on either side, known as Panamint Dry Lake.

In 1900 the mines surrounding Ballarat were at their peak. The Old Be Joyful, Ratcliff, World Beater, and Gem were turning out bullion worth $500,000. Few could imagine that one year later, many of the town's 300 residents would move 150 miles north to Tonapah, which seemed to offer even greater promise. When the Ratcliff Mine began to decline, there was little reason to remain. In 1917 the post office closed and Ballarat became a ghost town. Today, despite the exodus that began more than a hundred years ago, the town still lingers, recalling its past.

Ballarat, established in 1897 as a mining camp and supply center for the gold and silver mines located on the western slopes of the Panamint Mountains, was named for a well-known gold producing area in Australia. In its heyday Ballarat had a population of 500 hardy souls, a Wells Fargo station, post office, school, jail, morgue, three hotels, and seven saloons. It also had a red-light district featuring half a dozen cribs.

Today little is left of the town. There's a restored jail and a general store operated today by a Bureau of Land Management representative. The store offers showers as well as a porch where you can escape the sun, rest, and look about. On the day of our visit, the storekeeper had left a note: "Gone to town

# Ballarat Ghost Town

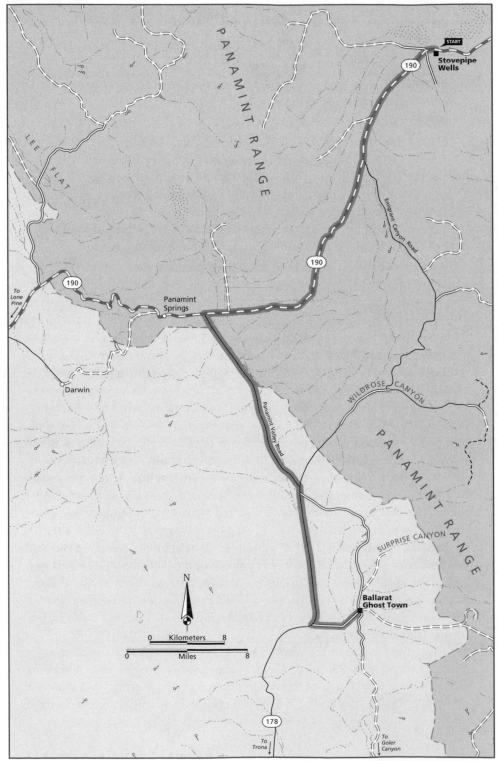

PANAMINT RANGE

LEE FLAT

START

190

Stovepipe Wells

Emigrant Canyon Road

190

190

To Lone Pine

Panamint Springs

Darwin

Panamint Valley Road

WILDROSE CANYON

PANAMINT RANGE

SURPRISE CANYON

N

Ballarat Ghost Town

0    Kilometers    8

0    Miles    8

178

To Trona

To Goler Canyon

for supplies—back soon. Enjoy the porch." There is also a graveyard with a number of unmarked graves, although one contains an epitaph worth lingering over. The marker of Seldom Seen Slim reads

CHARLES FERGE

PROSPECTER

SELDOM SEEN SLIM

1889–1968

"ME LONELY? HELL NO!

I'M HALF COYOTE AND HALF WILD BURRO!"

Ballarat also boasts a campground for $1.50 per person. It obviously offers peace and quiet—unless the ghosts stir at night.

It's rather difficult to discern what the ruins of the other buildings (constructed of mud and stone) might once have been. No one was at home on the day of our visit, or we might have been able to find out more history.

About 2 miles directly north of Ballarat, on the dirt road leading from town paralleling the mountains, lies the trailhead into Surprise Canyon. By hiking an old jeep route through here for about 5 miles one-way, you can access Panamint City, now a ghost town, located just inside the park's western border. The hike is popular.

The Panamint Valley is sometimes a flyway for very low-flying fighter planes. In the Southwest between Los Angeles and San Diego and extending more than 250 miles to the east are seven military installations with a flying mission. Each installation has men and women who are required to maintain their skills and test their equipment on a continuing basis. The California Desert Protection Act, passed by Congress in 1994, requires the integration of diverse missions through the protection of resources while ensuring the military's ability to conduct operations. Congress passed the Act to "preserve unrivaled scenic, geologic, and wildlife values associated with these unique natural landscapes." Congress also recognized that "continued use of the lands and airspace in the California desert region is essential for military purposes." We mention this so that you won't be too startled when a plane flies almost directly overhead. The plane traffic is less on weekends.

# Panamint Dunes

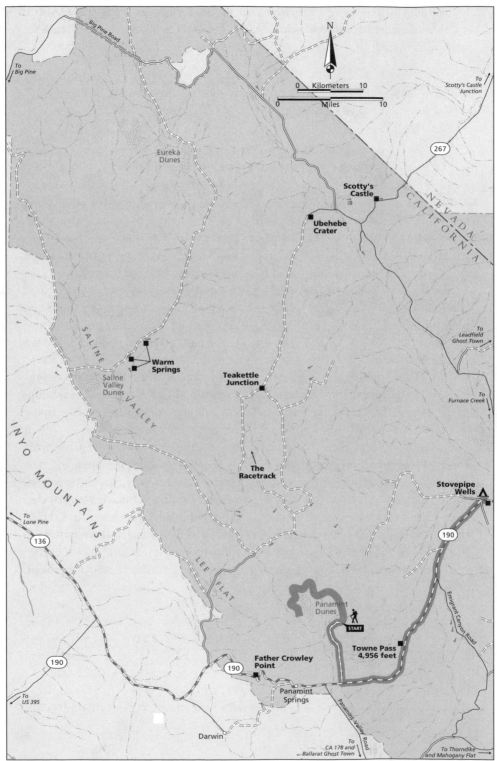

To Big Pine

Big Pine Road

Eureka Dunes

To Scotty's Castle Junction

NEVADA
CALIFORNIA

267

**Scotty's Castle**

**Ubehebe Crater**

SALINE VALLEY

**Warm Springs**

Saline Valley Dunes

**Teakettle Junction**

To Leadfield Ghost Town

To Furnace Creek

**The Racetrack**

INYO MOUNTAINS

**Stovepipe Wells**

To Lone Pine

136

190

LEE FLAT

190

**Father Crowley Point**

Panamint Dunes

START

Emigrant Canyon Road

**Towne Pass 4,956 feet**

190

To US 395

Panamint Springs

Darwin

Panamint Valley Road

To CA 178 and Ballarat Ghost Town

To Thorndike and Mahogany Flat

N

Kilometers 0 10
Miles 0 10

# 27 - Panamint Dunes

**TYPE OF TRIP:** Easy to moderate hike (due to soft sand); a more strenuous 200- to 300-foot climb to the top of the dunes.

**DISTANCE:** Approximately 6- to 6.5-mile round-trip hike.

**MAPS:** Park handout map; National Geographic/Trails Illustrated Topo Map 221.

**DIRECTIONS:** From Stovepipe Wells Campground, follow California Highway 190 west for 27.5 miles. You will traverse Towne Pass (elevation 4,956 feet). As soon as it seems you have made the final descent of the pass, you'll see a sign on the right indicating NO OFF-ROAD TRAVEL. Just beyond this sign on the right is a rough dirt road. Signs indicate that you are entering a wildlife study area. Follow this road for approximately 5.6 miles to the start of the hike. Park where the road begins a hard cut to the right, leading to the Old Big Four Mine. The dunes are directly in front of you. Please remember—foot travel only after leaving the dirt road.

## Description

Five areas of beautiful dunes lie within Death Valley. Four of these areas were designated as wilderness in 1994. Dunes often signify desert to many people, but only 1 percent of Death Valley's desert is dunes. The wind blows often here, flinging the sand, but to form dunes the shifting sand must be trapped somewhere.

All other dunes in Death Valley rise from flat valley floors, but the Panamint Dunes are perfectly situated on a slope at the horseshoe-shaped end of the Panamint Valley. They can be seen from the highway, but it's much better to hike to them through the desert wilderness. To the east of this valley lie the rugged Panamints, the snowy summit of Telescope Peak high above all. To the west is the Nelson Range, backed farther west by the towering Inyo Mountains. The area here is dotted by creosote and desert scrub.

Lizards (too swift to be identified) scamper about, and kangaroo rat tracks are visible near the numerous large and small burrows. Alluvial fans and bajadas spread from the canyons in the Panamints.

The walk to the dunes is a slight ascent through soft sand, but it is possible to find hard-packed areas to traverse, which leaves less impact. Upon reaching the first significant rise (at a little over 2,000 feet) you'll often encounter a breeze. This is a good place for a short break to gaze down the valley to the southeast. Directly in front of you is a rise called Lake Hill. Seeing the salt beds that surround it, it's easy to imagine the lake that existed here perhaps 10,000

*Hiking out of Panamint Dunes, near Panamint Springs.*

years ago—fairly recently in geological terms. In fact, there may have been water in this valley a mere 2,000 years ago, during a minor ice age.

It's a short, huffing hike to the top of the dunes, which are 200 to 300 feet high. Once you're there, the star shapes become obvious—and the view more spectacular.

On a negative note, the Panamint Valley is a fly-over and fly-through area for fighter planes from the military bases surrounding Death Valley, and many flew over us the day of our hike. Low-flying aircraft are obviously disconcerting to a wilderness experience, but the situation is apparently unavoidable.

# 28 - Father Crowley Point

**TYPE OF TRIP:** Drive.

**DISTANCE:** 37.3 miles from Stovepipe Wells; 8.8 miles from Panamint Springs.

**TYPE OF VEHICLE:** Passenger car.

**DIRECTIONS:** From Stovepipe Wells travel southwest on California Highway 190 for 28.5 miles to Panamint Springs. Drive north-north-west on CA 190 up a narrow, winding, mountain road for 8.1 miles to the signed viewpoint on the right. Go 0.7 mile down a rough dirt road to the actual viewpoint.

**MAPS:** Park handout map; National Geographic/Trails Illustrated Topo Map 221.

## Description

As you turn into the viewpoint, a sign reads: PADRE CROWLEY POINT. IN MEMORY OF THE PADRE OF THE DESERT. 1891–1940 . . . HE PASSED THIS WAY. Even from this brief epitaph, you get the feeling that Father Crowley was a wonderful man, and you can imagine him wandering the deserts in and around Death Valley, bringing prayers and friendship to the people who lived here.

The point offers incredible views from an elevation of 4,000 feet. Every desert color is on display. Your eyes sweep the Panamint Valley, the Panamint Dunes, Telescope Peak, Wildrose Peak, and the road over Towne Pass. You can see into the Darwin Hills, the Darwin Wilderness area, and the Argus Range to the south.

This is a short trip from Panamint Springs, but it's well worth mentioning here. Photographic opportunities in early morning and late afternoon are wonderful. In addition, the scene before you gives a good perspective to the breadth and scope of the area.

# Father Crowley Point

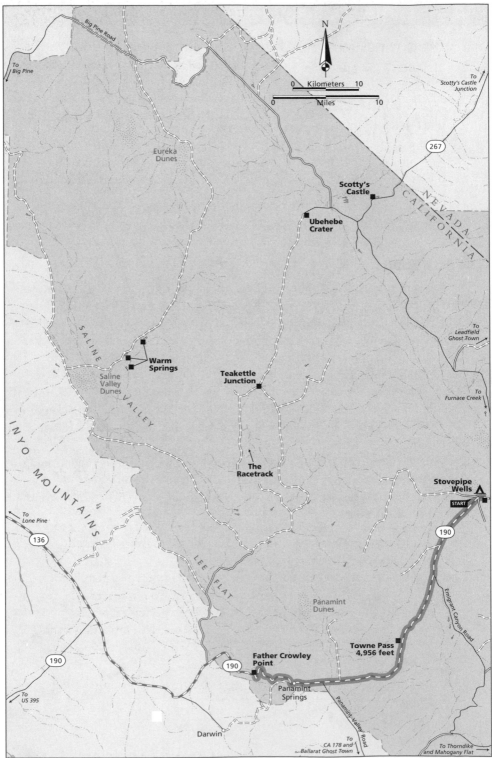

To Big Pine

Big Pine Road

Eureka Dunes

N

Kilometers 10
0
Miles
0        10

To Scotty's Castle Junction

267

NEVADA / CALIFORNIA

Scotty's Castle

Ubehebe Crater

To Leadfield Ghost Town

SALINE VALLEY

Warm Springs

Saline Valley Dunes

Teakettle Junction

To Furnace Creek

INYO MOUNTAINS

The Racetrack

Stovepipe Wells

START

To Lone Pine

136

LEE FLAT

190

Emigrant Canyon Road

190

Panamint Dunes

To US 395

190

Father Crowley Point

Towne Pass 4,956 feet

Panamint Springs

Panamint Valley Road

Darwin

To CA 178 and Ballarat Ghost Town

To Thorndike and Mahogany Flat

**TYPE OF TRIP:** An out-and-back backcountry drive on dirt and gravel roads, from whichever starting point you choose. Plan to devote a long, full day; take food, water, sun protection, a camera, and plenty of gas. There are no services in the area, so make sure your vehicle is in good shape. Ideally, you might want to take a tent along and spend the night at the base of the dunes. *NOTE:* In a flash flood, roads to the dunes may be impassable.

**DISTANCE:** We elected to make this trip from outside Death Valley, beginning in the California town of Big Pine, located about 90 miles north of Panamint Springs. Even though it might seem a distance to go, the trip is fantastic. The route takes you through the town of Lone Pine, where you are literally at the base of Mt. Whitney in the Sierra Nevada Mountains. If you begin your visit at Big Pine, the entire out and back trip is about 99 miles. If you travel within the park on the Ubehebe Crater Road (located 5.7 miles west of Scotty's Castle), an extremely rough road for at least the first 20 miles, the out-and-back distance is 86 miles.

**TYPE OF VEHICLE:** If you're driving to the dunes from Big Pine, a passenger car will work fine. If you make the trip from the road departing from Ubehebe Crater, you will want to consider a high-clearance, four-wheel-drive vehicle. In either case, trailers are not recommended.

**DIRECTIONS:** From within the park, go 5.7 miles west of Scotty's Castle to the Big Pine Road on your right (northwest). After 32.6 miles turn south onto the Eureka Dunes Road. Go 10.7 miles to the dunes.

From Big Pine go east on California Highway 168 for 2 miles to Death Valley Road on the right (southeast). At Mile 13.5 you'll see the Saline Valley Road on the right; stay on Death Valley Road. At 16.8 miles you will enter Death Valley National Park. This portion of the road is paved and winds through canyons, forests of juniper trees, and then a forest of Joshua trees. Soon the road drops into the remote Eureka Valley, a wilderness area.

At Mile 37.3 turn right onto a signed dirt road leading to Eureka Dunes. Follow this road for 10 miles and Eureka! You have arrived.

If you continue on the paved road, you will go through Hanging Rock Canyon and find Crater Mine. This road continues to Crankshaft Junction and then to Death Valley National Park and Scotty's Castle at the northeast end of the park.

**MAPS:** Park handout map; National Geographic/Trails Illustrated Topo Map 221.

# Eureka Sand Dunes

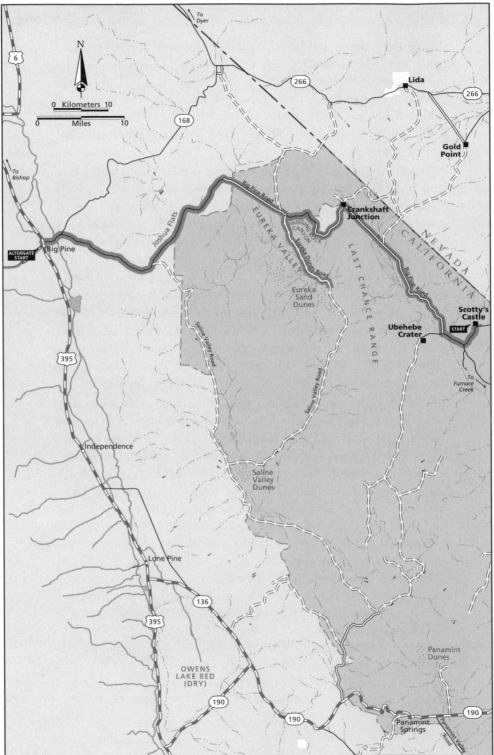

## Description

The 10,000-year-old Eureka Sand Dunes became part of Death Valley National Park in 1994 when new areas were added to the newly created national park. Death Valley now boasts the tallest dunes in California and the second tallest in North America. Only Colorado's Great Sand Dunes are taller.

As you drive toward the dunes, they don't seem all that large—they cover an area of only 3 miles long by 1 mile wide. But when you arrive at the base of the dunes, their enormity is apparent—and becomes even more apparent when you set off to hike to the 600 to 700 feet to the summit.

The setting is lovely, so lovely it's often hard to do the place justice. The Saline Range rises to the west, and the very high Last Chance Mountains lie to the east. Lying to the north are the White Mountains.

When you arrive you might see why many opt to camp. There are several parking areas and simple camping spots. Pit toilets are available, but there is no water here. The dunes are closed to dogs, off-road vehicles, and, to protect endangered plants that grow on the dunes, sandboards.

The dunes are popular for several good reasons. First, they sing! You can hear this phenomenon by hiking to the top of the dunes. If the sand is totally dry, when granules slide down the steep face, a very low, very deep sound can be heard. The mystery lies in why the sand won't sing when it's damp. Some say

*Eureka Sand Dunes, the park's largest, pose challenges for hikers, addressed by this couple with ski poles.*

the sounds are produced by the friction of sand granules sliding against one another.

Hearing the singing is not all that common, for the Eureka Dunes are often quite damp (even though they feel dry). Because Eureka Dunes lie in an area of mountains that capture storms, more rainfall occurs here than at other dunes.

In this isolated, fragile ecosystem, endemic species of plants and animals that exist nowhere else in the world manage to make this sand island home. Five species of endemic beetles and three plant species live here. Eureka dunegrass lives mainly on the higher slopes and has a solid root system as well as spines on the leaves. The Eureka Dunes evening primrose shows its white flowers at night. Shining milkvetch is covered with shining hairs to ward off heat and retain any moisture available. In very dry years, plants may not be visible. Most plants and animals live near the base of the dunes, so tread carefully as you explore.

Few animals can survive here, but you'll see many tracks in the sand. During our visit we were treated to the rare sight of a kangaroo rat hopping among the dunes.

You may explore at will on and around the dunes. A faint road track goes south around the dunes, but if you proceed you may need four-wheel drive. *Hint:* Use two-wheel drive for exploring, relying on four-wheel drive to extricate you from trouble.

As day fades into evening, the changing light plays dramatically on the dunes and the Last Chance Mountains. The dunes glow golden, and the contours soften like velvet folds. This is indeed a must-do trip for all ages.

## 30 - Devil's Hole–Ash Meadows National Wildlife Refuge

**TYPE OF TRIP:** Drive and walk.

**DISTANCE:** 38 miles one way.

**TYPE OF VEHICLE:** Passenger car.

**DIRECTIONS:** Take California Highway 190 east from Furnace Creek to California Highway 127 and turn right. Go about 300 feet to Stateline Road and turn left. Go 7 miles to a gravel road signed ASH MEADOWS WILDLIFE REFUGE and turn left. Drive 4.4 miles to a T intersection and turn right. Go 1.5 miles to the parking area.

## Description

What is a pupfish? The dictionary defines pupfish as "any of several tiny, stout killifishes of the genus *Cyprinodon*, inhabiting marshy waters in arid areas of western North America." Several species are endangered.

Although pupfish live in a variety of desert areas, including Texas and New Mexico, they once lived in Death Valley's Lake Manly, some 15,000 years ago. As Lake Manly began to recede and began to increase in salinity, pupfish had to adapt. To do so, pupfish had to use the biological phenomenon known as osmosis—the process wherein a substance of greater concentration passes to an area of lower concentration through a semipermeable membrane—but in reverse.

In all living creatures with kidneys, the semipermeable membranes are called glomeruli. Glomeruli in freshwater fish remove impurities from body fluids and, through osmosis, secrete those impurities in the form of dilute uric acid. That's not the case with pupfish that live in salt water. These pupfish gulp salt water and, through reverse osmosis, secrete highly concentrated salt water to maintain a proper balance in their body fluids.

The ancient pupfish survives today because of concerted efforts by many individuals and groups to save this 2- to 3-inch minnowlike fish. In the Death Valley area, there are four species and three endemic subspecies of pupfish, several of which descended from ancestors of the Lake Manley stock. These include the Salt Creek pupfish found only at Salt Creek, north of Furnace

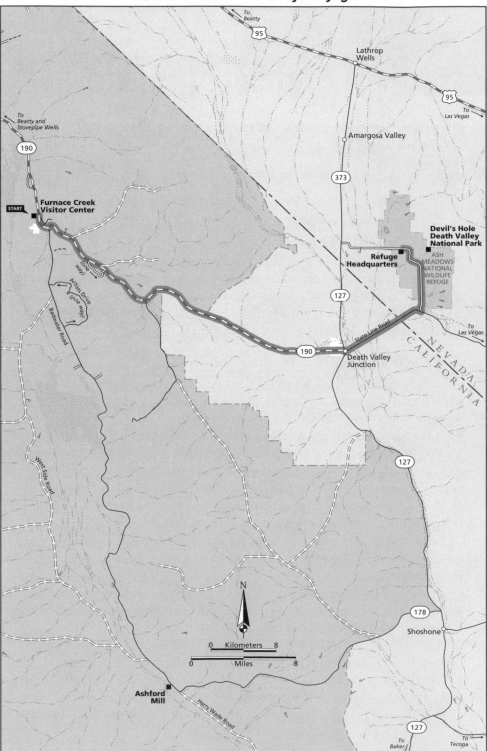

Creek; the Cottonball Marsh pupfish; and the Saratoga Springs pupfish. The Amargosa pupfish is found in Amargosa Canyon.

Three other species are found in Nevada in Devil's Hole, a detached unit of Death Valley National Park. Devil's Hole is within the Ash Meadows National Wildlife Refuge, a forty-acre complex that is home to the Devil's Hole pupfish, the Ash Meadows pupfish, and the Warm Springs pupfish.

Although pupfish live in a variety of areas throughout the Southwest, they are not known to exist anywhere else in the world—and that is what makes their survival in Death Valley so vital. Scientists believe that the ancestors of the valley's pupfish lived 15,000 years ago in Lake Manly. When that dried up, they adapted from deep and cold and freshwater environs to the warm saltwater environs of today.

The Devil's Hole pupfish have been totally isolated for 10,000 to 20,000 years longer than any other pupfish in Death Valley. Their environment is a water-filled cavern well over 500 feet deep. Here the water is salty and the temperature remains at 92° Fahrenheit. A rock ledge near the surface serves as their feeding and spawning area. If the primary food, algae, is abundant, their numbers range from 300 to 500 in summer. Barn owls nest in the cave and drop their pellets into the water, enhancing the water's nutrients, which promotes algae growth. The conclusion? Owls are good for pupfish!

Unfortunately, the history of Ash Meadows has been contentious. In 1967 the Devil's Hole pupfish officially became an endangered species. At the same time, farming came to the area and the cavern began to lose water as farmers used it for wells and irrigation. In 1970 scientists were forced to make an artificial feeding shelf, with lighting, but the pupfish would not use it. In 1971 a federal court ordered the cessation of water pumping, and in 1976 the U.S. Supreme Court reverted water rights to Devil's Hole, since it had been part of a national monument since 1952. Then in 1977 a development company proposed a subdivision of 30,000 lots. Fortunately, in 1981 Sen. Alan Cranston (D–California) wrote legislation proposing that the area be designated as the Desert Pupfish National Wildlife Refuge. Then the Nature Conservancy bought out the developer and sold the land to the U.S. Fish and Wildlife Service. They, in turn, wrote a recovery plan for the entire area. In the end, with many factions working toward saving the pupfish, Ash Meadows became a national wildlife refuge in 1984. Today, not only are there pupfish in Devil's Hole but the area also contains twenty-six species of endemic plants and animals.

The Ash Meadows complex lies east of Death Valley National Park, in Nevada. Viewing the pupfish is often difficult, since visitors do not have entry to the "hole" itself. But a trip to Ash Meadows, about 43 miles one-way from Furnace Creek Visitor Center, is interesting and well worth adding to your list of places to explore.

# Appendix A
## Suggestions for Further Hikes, Explorations, and Activities

This book obviously does not cover all that Death Valley offers. We've attempted to include places that might be appropriate for everyone and hope that our suggestions have given you ideas for further exploring on your own. Most of all, we hope you enjoy this park as much as we do and that your exploring leads to special discoveries.

## The Saline Valley

For a real adventure and incredible beauty, drive the Saline Valley Road. This exploration requires a high-clearance vehicle and often four-wheel drive, especially in winter. It is probably best if drivers are experienced in off-road travel. The road may be closed due to rain and washouts, so be sure to check with rangers before embarking on this venture. Have a good topographical map of the area such as Trails Illustrated/National Geographic Topo Map 221, as well as USGS quad maps. Other essentials include lots of gas and drinking water, a shovel, flashlight, and food. Many folks take camping gear; the road is long and slow—and a night or several nights spent camping beneath the desert sky in this area is a unique experience. For safety's sake, be sure to tell others of your plans before you head out.

Begin at Panamint Springs on California Highway 190. Go 13.7 miles west on CA 190, and then turn right (northeast) onto the road to Lee Flat. Go 8 miles on this road until you come to a huge Joshua tree forest, and then follow the sign for the Saline Valley Road (a left turn), which goes north.

Now that you're on the road, travel as far as you wish. It is 78 miles one-way to the paved road to Big Pine.

As noted, the first treat is the Joshua tree forest. The Inyo Mountains lie to the west, and there are many opportunities here to do some wilderness hiking.

About halfway through the drive (39 miles), you'll come to the salt marsh, on your right. Shortly thereafter, on your right again, are the Saline Valley Dunes. Because the mountains are so high (nearly 10,000 feet), the low dunes are hard to discern, even though they spread over a large area. Just beyond the dunes is a four-wheel-drive road leading to the east (right), and it is on this road that the warm springs lie.

Ultimately the Saline Valley Road will bring you onto a paved road; go west to the town of Big Pine. If you're returning to Death Valley, you can travel by paved road all the way. Take U.S. Highway 395 south to Lone Pine, and then take California Highway 136 south to the junction with CA 190 east to Death Valley.

## Saratoga Spring and the Ibex Dunes

Saratoga Spring and Ibex Dunes are 91 miles one-way from Furnace Creek Visitor Center or 64 miles one-way from Death Valley Junction. The Saratoga Spring area invites a visit; it is a quiet, cool place, perfect for reflection and surrounded by hills and beauty. Saratoga Spring is located in the extreme southeast corner of the park. Except for the last 10 unpaved miles, it is not a difficult trip.

Take California Highway 190 southeast from Furnace Creek Visitor Center to Death Valley Junction. Go south on California Highway 127 for 28 miles to Shoshone. Continue south on CA 127 for 24 miles, where CA 127 turns east and a graded dirt road goes west. Take a right (west) onto the graded dirt road and go 6 miles; turn right (north) on the first dirt road and go 4 miles to Saratoga Spring. Check with rangers on road conditions before starting out.

Before reaching the spring you'll cross the Amargosa River, once a major watercourse, which still carries water into Death Valley.

Three ponds, which contain water year-round, provide seasonal bases for migratory birds, including the coot. One species of pupfish, *Cyprinodon nevadensis nevadensis*, lives year-round in the ponds. These are a different subspecies from the pupfish in Salt Creek.

The Ibex Dunes, which cannot be seen from the paved roads, lie about 1.5 miles due east of Saratoga Spring. You can hike to them from the Saratoga Spring Road. The dunes are home to the Mojave fringe-toed lizard.

Mountain biking is allowed on the many miles of paved roads that are open to the public and on dirt roads (there are plenty of those!). Bikers cannot travel cross-country or on hiking trails. Check with the visitor center or ranger stations for current road conditions and maps—do not bike into canyons if storms threaten. You can pick up handouts listing ride ratings, from easiest to more difficult.

Photographic opportunities abound in Death Valley, and you'll soon see how the colors change, soften, and glow, depending on the time of day or evening. Sunrise photography (be there early) is great at the Death Valley Dunes, Dante's View, Zabriskie Point, and Badwater, just to mention a few spots. Sunsets can be spectacular, but they're short; again, arrive in a timely fashion. Best places to be late in the day include Death Valley Dunes, Artists Drive, Zabriskie Point, Ubehebe Crater, Golden Canyon, and the Salt Flats.

Drive and then take short walks to look for plants and special rocks, being aware of the admonition that all rocks belong to the "leverite" class ("Leave 'er right there."). Early and late in the day are good times to see wildlife. Birding is another fascinating way to spend some hours.

Backpacking is popular in Death Valley in the cooler months. But remember how much water weighs, and be aware of how much you must carry (one gallon—about eight pounds—per person, per day minimum). There are no reliable water sources in the backcountry. Most of the hikes are cross-country routes. Free backcountry camping permits are available at Furnace Creek Visitor Center and ranger stations. Suggested trips include Hungry Bill's Ranch, Hanaupah Canyon, Hole-in-the-Wall, Indian Pass, Surprise Canyon, Fall Canyon, and Cottonwood–Marble Canyon Loop. The visitor center can provide you with a complete list, as well as updates on current conditions.

## Death Valley '49ers

Each November the Death Valley '49ers recall in a celebration the hardships endured by early pioneers. That the gathering has been a great success since its inception in 1949 speaks well for the people involved—and for their objectives.

"The purpose of the Death Valley '49ers is to promote understanding and appreciation of Death Valley and its history," states the written goal of this group, but their involvement in Death Valley is much more. The group "fosters appreciation of Death Valley as a rare desert environment having unique natural and cultural histories...." Much focus is placed on that persevering group of pioneers of 1849–1850 who survived incredible winter hardships in Death Valley while on their way to the California gold fields. In recognition of the spirit and will of these families, each November the Death Valley '49ers work closely with Death Valley National Park personnel and with the park's mission. Each year, the encampment event draws thousands of people to this beautiful place. In addition, the '49ers maintain and distribute a scholarship endowment fund, providing monies to qualifying local high school students to further their education. This amazing group manages to do a lot, considering they are a nonprofit volunteer organization. The fee to join the '49ers (and they welcome new members) is $20 per year per couple.

The annual encampment runs for a week or so. Those in attendance will be treated to an amazing array of options. A small sampling includes photography, woodcarving and needlework competitions; an invitational Western show; several four-by-four trips; dancing and live music; an old-time fiddle contest; tours of historic places in the park; true and funny stories relating to the park and its people; slide shows; mystery hikes; a pioneer costume contest; films; and a golf tournament. This sampling should be enough to entice all to join.

For information, visit the Web at www.deathvalley49ers.org, or write Death Valley '49ers, 10254 Monterey Street, Bellflower, CA 90706-6732.

# Appendix B
## Lodging and Campgrounds

Death Valley National Park offers three choices for lodging, all of which are located conveniently to different areas of the park.

**Furnace Creek Ranch** is adjacent to the Furnace Creek Visitor Center, centrally located on California Highway 190. Inside the family-oriented setting, you'll find the Borax Museum, a motel, a swimming pool, a golf course with pro shop, a post office, a general store, bars and restaurants, tennis courts, and other amenities. Elegant **Furnace Creek Inn**, in operation since 1927, is about 1.5 miles south of the Ranch on CA 190. The inn provides luxury accommodations and is wheelchair-accessible. Here you'll find pools, gardens, tennis courts, golf, horseback riding, and fine dining. For reservations call (800) 236–7916 or (760) 786–2345. Both the ranch and the inn are open year-round, and both are owned by Xanterra Parks and Resorts.

**Stovepipe Wells** is a park concession that offers nice motel rooms (wheelchair-accessible), a swimming pool, laundry, gift store, and bar and restaurant and a gas station/convenience store across the road. It is located on CA 190, 14 miles west of the intersection with California Highway 374 (to Beatty, Nevada) and Scotty's Castle Road. RV hookups are available. For reservations and information call (760) 786–2387.

**Panamint Springs Resort** is privately owned and is located on CA 190 about 30 miles west of Stovepipe Wells (you travel over Towne Pass) at the western central edge of the park. Motel rooms are available as well as RV hookups, a restaurant/bar, showers, and a gas station. The campground is in a lovely setting, with trees and bushes offering shade, plus a great view of the Panamint Valley. Call (775) 482–7680 for reservations and information. The resort is open year-round.

Lodging outside the park is available at most surrounding towns. East of the park you'll find motels in Tonopah, Beatty, Amargosa Valley, and Pahrump, Nevada, and Shoshone and Baker, California. West of Death Valley, lodging is available in Bishop, Big Pine, Lone Pine, Olancha, Ridgecrest, and Inyokern, California.

Nine campgrounds dot the park.

**Furnace Creek Campground,** located on CA 190 about 0.5 mile north of the visitor center, is open year-round. At an elevation of –196 feet and with 136 sites, this campground offers water, tables, some trees, firepits, flush toilets, a dump station—and a few walk-in tent sites. Camping fee is $16 per night, $10 per night from April to October. For reservations (make them well in advance), call (800) 365–2267 or visit reservations.nps.gov. Group sites are also available here with reservations.

**Sunset Campground** is just across CA 190 from Furnace Creek Campground. Primarily it's an RV campground. Here, too, the elevation is –196 feet. Sunset boasts 1,000 sites on asphalt and is open October through April. The camping fee is $10 per night. Water, flush toilets, and a dump station are available.

**Texas Spring Campground** sits above Sunset Campground at sea level and has ninty-two sites at $12 per night. This campground is open October through April and offers water, tables, firepits, flush toilets, and a dump station. In the busy spring season, this campground may set limits on RV use to accommodate tent space.

Also sitting at sea level is **Stovepipe Wells Campground**, north and west of the above mentioned sites on CA 190, 9 miles south of the junction with Scotty's Castle Road. The campground is open October through April and charges a $10 nightly fee. There are 190 sites, some with tables and firepits. Water, flush toilets, and a dump station are available. Adjacent to the park campground, a private campground operated by the park concessions provides a few RV sites with hookups.

**Emigrant Campground** is located 8 miles southwest of Stovepipe Wells on CA 190. Perched at 2,100 feet, Emigrant is open year-round. There are ten sites with water, tables, and flush toilets. This free campground is for tents only.

**Mesquite Spring Campground** is at 1,800 feet elevation and is open year-round. Thirty sites are available here at $10 per night. Water, tables, firepits, flush toilets, and a dump station are provided. The campground is 2 miles down the road from the Grapevine Ranger Station. Turn south off Scotty's Castle Road just before the ranger station. This is the most northern campground in the park and is about 43 miles north of Furnace Creek, conveniently located near Scotty's Castle and Ubehebe Crater.

**Wildrose Campground** is located about 13 miles south of Stovepipe Wells on Emigrant Canyon Road. At an elevation of 4,100 feet, this no-fee campground is open year-round and offers twenty-three sites with water, tables, firepits, and pit toilets.

**Thorndike** (six sites) and **Mahogany Flat** (ten sites) campgrounds are accessible by high-clearance vehicles; four-wheel drive may be necessary. Both are free and offer tables, firepits, and pit toilets but no water. Both campgrounds are open March to November and are often used by those hiking up to Telescope Peak.

Backcountry camping is allowed in some areas; free permits, obtained at the visitor center or any ranger station, are required. Current rules state that backcountry camping is allowed 2 miles from a developed area, a paved road, or a day-use area. Campsites must be 100 yards from any water source. Camping *is not allowed* on the following dirt roads: Titus Canyon, West Side, Wildrose, Skidoo, and Aguereberry Point Roads; the first 8 miles of Cottonwood Canyon Road; and Racetrack Road from Teakettle Junction to Homestake Dry Camp. Camping is not allowed at Keane Wonder Mine, Lost Burro Mine, or Ubehebe Lead Mine. Check with rangers to be certain the area you wish to use is open for camping. Fires are prohibited in the backcountry; backpack stoves are recommended.

# Appendix C
## Sample List of Ranger Nature Walks and Talks

Ranger-led walks are sometimes available, but not necessarily on a reoccurring basis. Check at the visitor center for specifics. Past walks have included Scotty's Castle (Living History Tours daily), Mosaic Canyon, Gower Gulch, Golden Canyon, Texas Springs, Desert Solitudes Hike, Harmony Borax, Canyon Secrets, and the Sand Dunes. Check at the visitor center for weekly schedules.

Programs offered (usually at Furnace Creek Auditorium) include such topics as:

| | |
|---|---|
| 101 Ways to Die in Death Valley | Weather Extremes |
| Bad Habitats | Geologic Marvels |
| Death Valley in 1849 | Death Valley Birding—Getting Started |
| The Death Valley Railroad | Ghost Highways |
| Behind the Scenes | Wheelers, Pointers, and Leaders |
| Colorful Characters | Desert Bighorn |
| Desert Wilderness | Goodwater |
| Weather Extremes | Two Castles |
| Flash Flood! | Death Valley on Foot |
| Boron: The Light Heavyweight | Death Valley Vignettes |

Death Valley National Park issues rules and guidelines, expecting that visitors will learn and follow them. Following is a short summary of regulations designed to help protect both the park and visitors:

- Driving and bike riding off-road is prohibited. Bikes are not permitted on trails, closed roads, or in wilderness areas. The desert is an extremely fragile place, easily damaged and slow to recover.

- Removing rocks, artifacts, plants, or animals is prohibited, as is the use of metal detectors.

- Do not feed any wildlife.

- Pets are allowed in developed areas and on park roads, provided they are leashed at all times. No pets are allowed in wilderness areas or on trails.

- Horses are not allowed in campgrounds, on roads, or on interpretive trails. Grazing is not allowed.

- When hiking or exploring, carry out all garbage. Human waste may be buried 6 inches deep and more than 200 yards from water sources. The park encourages people to carry out their own toilet paper, noting that many areas are being negatively impacted.

- All types of weapons are strictly prohibited.

- Obey the posted speed limits. Single-car accidents are the leading cause of death in Death Valley. Drivers are not aware of curves, hills, and narrow roads.

- Do not count on water from springs: They are often dry and probably contaminated. You'll need to carry at least one gallon of water per person for a one-day hike; plan to stash water if cross-country hiking. Because of intense heat and low humidity in Death Valley in summer, the park does not encourage hiking at low elevations in Badwater, canyons, and the valley floor. If you visit in summer, this is a good time to climb high—Telescope Peak or Wildrose Peak, for example.

- In winter, high elevations get a fair share of snow and ice. Winter travel requires safety equipment and proper clothing.

- Maintained trails are few in the park, so most hiking is on your own. Please practice low-impact hiking—desert vegetation is fragile.

- Be aware of rattlesnakes.
- Do not enter structures, tunnels, or shafts at the old mining areas. Check with a ranger to see if any mines are explorable.
- Flash floods occur in the park. If you are backcountry camping, do not set up camp in a drainage or dry wash.
- Be aware of hantavirus, a serious disease carried in the feces and urine of rodents. Stay out of dusty, rodent-inhabited buildings, and avoid rodent dens.

# Appendix E
## Suggested Reading Materials

*An Introduction to the Geology of Death Valley* by Michael Collier. Death Valley Natural History Association, Death Valley, California, 1990.

*Best Easy Day Hikes: Death Valley* by Bill Cunningham and Polly Burke. Falcon Publishing, Inc., Helena, Montana, 2000.

*A Naturalist's Death Valley* by Dr. Edmund C. Jaeger. Death Valley '49ers, Inc., Fifth Edition, North Hollywood Printing, Burbank, California, 1975.

*Death Valley National Park, an Interpretive History* by James W. Cornett. Companion Press, Santa Barbara, California, 1996.

*Death Valley—A Scenic Wonderland* by Steven L. Walker and Dorothy K. Hilburn. Canyonlands Publications, Bellemont, Arizona, 1995.

*Death Valley & the Amargosa—A Land of Illusion* by Richard E. Lingenfelter. University of California Press, Berkeley and Los Angeles, California, 1986.

*Death Valley, the Story Behind the Scenery* by Bill Clark. 2002 KC publications, Inc., Las Vegas, Nevada, 2002.

*Death Valley to Yosemite: Frontier Mining Camps & Ghost Towns* by L. Burr Belden and Mary DeDecker. Spotted Dog Press, Inc., Bishop, California, 2000.

*Deserts* by James A. MacMahon. The Audubon Society Nature Guides, Alfred A. Knopf, Inc., New York, New York, 1985.

*Exploring Death Valley* by Ruth Kirk. Stanford University Press, Stanford, California, 1968.

*Geology Underfoot in Death Valley and Owens Valley* by Robert P. Sharp and Allen F. Glazner. Mountain Press, Missoula, Montana, 1997.

*Wild Country Companion* by Will Harmon. Falcon Press Publishing Co., Inc., Helena, Montana, 1994.

*Wildflowers of Death Valley National Park and the Mojave Desert* by Death Valley Natural History Association, Death Valley, California, 1999.

## Maps

Death Valley National Park, California/Nevada, USA; Trails Illustrated/National Geographic Topographic Map 221.

Free Death Valley National Park handout map.

Detailed topo maps as needed for hiking areas. These are available at Furnace Creek Visitor Center or from the Death Valley Natural History Association; (760) 786–3285.

## Death Valley National Park Contacts

Death Valley National Park
P.O. Box 579
Death Valley, CA 92328-0570
(760) 786–2331; www.nps.gov/deva

Death Valley Natural History Association
P.O. Box 188
Death Valley, CA 92328
(800) 478–8564; e-mail: devahstry@aol.com

Furnace Creek Visitor Center
(760) 786–3200; www.nps.gov/deva
Camping reservations:
(800) 365–CAMP

California Desert Web site:
www.californiadesert.gov

Panamint Springs Resort: (775) 482–7680

Stovepipe Wells Village: (760) 786–2387

Scotty's Castle: (760) 786–2392

Furnace Creek Inn & Ranch: (760) 786–2345

## About the Authors

Bert and Jane Gildart have written dozens of stories and books about America's national parks. Their work has appeared in *National Wildlife, Travel & Leisure, The Christian Science Monitor, Trailer Life*, as well as dozens of other publications and several FalconGuides. Death Valley is one of their favorite parks, and they generally spend a portion of each winter camping in the park, hiking the trails, and exploring the backcountry roads. When they are not traveling, they make their home in Montana.

# THE INSIDER'S SOURCE

With more than 540 West-related titles, we have the area covered. Whether you're looking for the path less traveled, a favorite place to eat, family-friendly fun, a breathtaking hike, or enchanting local attractions, our pages are filled with ideas to get you from one state to the next.

For a complete listing of all our titles, please visit our Web site at www.GlobePequot.com. The Globe Pequot Press is the largest publisher of local travel books in the United States and is a leading source for outdoor recreation guides.

# FOR BOOKS TO THE WEST